You are the architect of your future, not the tenant of your past

by Paul Gilbert

To Poppy and Jon with my love.

Published by:
LBC Wise Counsel

ISBN 9781838358938

Copyright © 2022 Paul Gilbert

All rights reserved. No part of this publication may be reproduced, stored in a retrieval system, or transmitted, in any form or by any means without the prior permission in writing of the publisher.

This book is sold subject to the condition that it shall not, by way of trade or otherwise, be lent, resold, hired out or otherwise circulated without the publisher's prior consent in any form other than that supplied by the publisher.

British Library Cataloguing in Publication Data available.

I am very grateful for the care, design and thoughtfulness of Jon Honeyford and Oomph Design for their work on this and my previous books.

Introduction

Writing my regular Sunday blog has become a gentle therapy for my spinning mind, a chance to rest my thoughts on a nice new blank page and to let them breathe without me. Bringing these posts into a book each year has also become a familiar routine. This is the 2022 collection. If you are a regular reader of my online blogs, I hope you will find some old friends within these pages, and if you are new to my words, I hope there is a gentle care in the thoughts I have shared that you will feel and enjoy.

The cover design is, as always, by the brilliant Jon Honeyford of Oomph Design in Cheltenham. This cover is especially evocative for me as the space in which I find my own thoughts is sometimes less comfortable than I would like, but I also know that there is always light. Jon has captured that feeling so simply, but also so eloquently and with such care. The title for this collection is taken from one of the blogs. It is a phrase I use in much of my work and is about finding our own way; a chance to walk towards the light and not to dwell in the dark.

Thank you for being with me in my thoughts. I hope we may meet again in 2023. 😊

Take care. Paul xx

Contents

January 2022

The unfamiliar path	12
The Prime Minister, the waiter and the C-Suite breaker	15
For all of us, carrying our story	18
In quiet praise of our inner introvert	21

February 2022

Admiring "opponents"	25
The blank page	27
Do not conform to the pattern of this world, but be transformed by the renewing of your mind	30
Broken ribs	34
An armada of love in small boats of hope	37

March 2022

Read the room, see what is needed, and be the person who tries to meet the need	41
Memories will always ache, but the pain will fade and our difference will be made	44
We could be heroes	47
27 March 1962	51

April 2022

My hobbyhorse is not at the races	57
Ambition is the shape of you	60
Packing away the moments that make up some great days	63
A mentor	65

May 2022

The long walk into ignorance	69

June 2022

The follower's tale	71
Leadership is	73
The seventy-five-year career	75
The hurtling blur	79

July 2022

For the pixels	82
About a blog	86
The great bacon roll debacle	89
How much does an email weigh?	92

August 2022

A quiet reflection on love and gratitude	96

September 2022

Together again	99
Gifts that tell your story	101

October 2022

What matters...	105
From Baker Street to Moorgate, a needle pulling thread	108
Leadership ain't easy, but...	110
Above all, we must do no harm	114
The ODPS System explained	117
Where are you from?	121

November 2022

It's about being strategic, innit?!	125
Seeing the good for the trees	128
You are the architect of your future, not the tenant of your past	131
On our watch, our scandal	134

December 2022

If sadness casts a shadow in the sun's low light	137
Acceptance	139

January 2022:

The unfamiliar path

It's January, and another year (thank goodness).

Wherever you are and however you feel, I hope this year unfolds with kindness and care. I am long past wanting to heap pressure on myself (or anyone else) with ambitious promises to lose weight, start a new hobby or to sort out the loft; and certainly not to engage in anything wearing Lycra and the inevitable pastry-wrapped-in-clingfilm look. However, I do hope to continue to write regularly in this place.

If you will come with me, I would like us to go to places where we can gently stroll around what kindness and care means for us. I also expect to clamber onto an occasional cathartic rant if we find that dumb knobbery still hangs in the air. I hope we may also rest our bigger thoughts in deeper, gentler waters to allow our weary hopes some peace and calm.

If you will come with me, I hope to avoid wading through the platitudes and clichés about change that we have all heard before. Instead, I want to focus, simply and deliberately, on noticing how things are. The problem with change messages is that we assume we know their meaning because we have heard them a thousand times before. We have cloaked them in plain sight where their truth is now muffled and obscure. However, if we can pause enough to properly notice what is happening around us, we might just see their truth again, with fresh eyes and an open mind.

Noticing is therefore the key, but to notice we need to bring ourselves into the moment; like taking an unfamiliar path to a familiar destination and then remembering more of what we have seen along the way.

The unfamiliar path will help us to notice that it's not normal or healthy for our work to make us unhappy; work should be a place to feel valued and purposeful. It will help us to notice that it's not normal or healthy for relationships to undermine us, and that we should not make excuses for how others treat us. And instead of feeling that we have not been heard, we will notice that it is not normal or healthy to hide our needs in heroic stoicism. We have hopes and fears and we need to talk about both.

The unfamiliar path might help us to notice that we could change the way we behave; it might encourage us to do something different or new; and it might help us to find a voice for our needs, rather than hoping that others will notice what we have failed to say out loud.

This unfamiliar path is therefore the start of noticing the things we should not accept from others, while at the same time learning to notice when we can be more accepting of ourselves. Accepting, for example, of the kind things that others say about us. And perhaps, just perhaps, realising that our self-esteem is not always a reliable witness to how others see our contribution or potential.

The unfamiliar path is not a metaphor for going away. If we can change things for the better and learn to accept that our daily self-critical commentary may not be what others think or say, it is just as likely to be a metaphor for wanting to stay.

Finding room in our stubborn ways to love ourselves a little more will be a far more precious gift to our future selves than anything we write in a CV seeking pastures new.

We all know it is a little too easy to say that the place where we will grow will happen next, when it should be now. The time to be amazing might indeed be one day in the future, but it is also today. And the chance to make a difference might never be perfect, but may be lost forever for waiting. Before there is change I know with certainty that we must first notice and then pause. My wish therefore for this New Year is to walk the unfamiliar path with you, so we can notice and pause together. Thank you for your company and for coming with me.

The Prime Minister, the waiter and the C-Suite breaker

A workplace culture is observable. It always happens in plain sight, and the most important people in maintaining a dysfunctional culture are those who enable the harm to continue.

It has been quite a week for our political elite. The Prime Minister's apology in Parliament has been dissected syllable by syllable and frame by frame. Whatever you think of him, his leadership or the situation, we have all now glimpsed his workplace culture and, I suggest, it is somewhat sub-optimal.

I occasionally need to vent my frustration and rant, but to be honest I feel too tired to make the effort. I don't have it in me to find a clever put-down or to take comfort in retweetable indignation. When we feel worn down by the relentlessness of a situation, we stop trying to find a solution and start to think about how we can just endure things until they pass.

Two groups emerge when there is such dysfunction. The first group (often small and senior, but nearly always invested in the status quo to meet their needs) will defend the achievements of the leader to excuse his failings. The second group (often larger, but much less powerful, and less invested) will seek change for a while, but when trying to change things fails, this group becomes diminished and exhausted.

If you have ever felt bullied at work, or if you are a person of colour or a woman who has felt side-lined, ignored or undermined (or worse) so that you felt diminished and exhausted by a workplace culture, I am certain you will also be able to point at those who kept the status quo intact and who made fighting against the harm seem pointless.

A workplace culture is observable. It always happens in plain sight, and the most important people in maintaining a dysfunctional culture are those who enable the harm to continue.

I was once invited to dinner in one of London's fanciest restaurants. The food looked amazing, but it was eye-wateringly expensive. I was the guest of a law firm partner, and I was his newly won client. The evening was memorable however not for the food, but for how rude the partner was to a young waiter. At one point in the evening, he called the waiter over and said loudly enough for many tables to hear "I said I wanted my coffee WITH my dessert. Are you DEAF or STUPID?"

I am rarely shocked, but for a few moments I was left utterly speechless. I sat back in my chair, gathered my thoughts, and told the partner quietly that I had made a mistake and that I would not be using the firm. He was of course immediately mortified and contrite. He blustered excuses about having had a stressful day and said he would leave a super generous tip, but I knew (as you do, reading this) that if he could behave like this in front of a newly won client, the behaviour behind closed doors would not be kind, thoughtful or caring. I also know that my small decision did nothing to change the culture of the firm. My host went on to be "award-winning", and a celebrated rainmaker in his firm, his harm enabled for more years to come by those excusing his weaknesses.

A workplace culture is observable. It always happens in plain sight, and the most important people in maintaining a dysfunctional culture are those who enable the harm to continue.

Just before Christmas I spoke to a General Counsel who had been informed that her chief executive had lost confidence in her judgement. This, as we know, is a pathetic and cowardly euphemism for being told he couldn't do something he wanted to do. She had decided to leave and was negotiating her exit. My sense, sadly, was that she was also now trying to manage her own crisis of confidence as well as the uncertainty of what happens next.

I have a great deal of concern for the well-being of senior in-house lawyers facing up to bullying executive colleagues. These hyper-competitive environments where there is often a personality cult around the chief executive, are incredibly destructive. So why does it keep happening? It happens because Boards, especially non-executive directors, do not see the chief executive as a conduct risk if he is hurting people, only if he is hurting shareholder value.

A workplace culture is observable. It always happens in plain sight, and the most important people in maintaining a dysfunctional culture are those who enable the harm to continue.

The Prime Minister, the client partner in the fancy restaurant and the bullying chief executive are not kept in power because of their gifts, but because their weaknesses are excused.

We can change this. It is not inevitable, but we need to notice the harm, and then we need to believe that stopping the harm is more important than continuing the apparent success.

For all of us, carrying our story

I do not have to manage through the symptoms or emotional impact of the menopause.

I am not black.

I do not have a broad regional accent in a room full of sophisticated sounding speakers.

I do not have to think if being gay is something I can discuss at work or should instead hold close.

I have not been pestered or harassed just because I am a woman.

I have not been bullied in a previous role.

I do not have to think if I am wearing too much make-up or not enough. I do not have to think if my heel is too high.

I have not returned to work from maternity leave to find I am unnoticed in a world running too fast for me to keep up.

I have not had to consider if my promotion is compatible with my complicated childcare arrangements.

I have not had to worry that my imposter self-commentary demands that I am perfect every day.

I have not had to plan the children's tea while creating a spreadsheet for my boss.

I have not had to think if starting a family is going to inconvenience my colleagues; or if not starting a family means that others judge me without a care for what I actually want or what I feel.

I have not arrived at work exhausted from a weekend fighting for support for my child with special educational needs or disability.

I do not carry the guilt of placing my elderly mum in a care home that looks after her needs but knowing it is not what she would have wanted.

We all carry a story. It is an all day, every day narrative that sits alongside every behaviour we reveal and every syllable we utter.

With all my advantages and privilege, and with all the blessings you can imagine, I am almost ashamed to say, that sometimes I can shrink into my own inadequacy and feel confidence and hope slip through my fingers.

We all carry a story that is never written on a CV.

Some things seem petty and go unmentioned because after all "isn't it the same for everyone, and everyone else seems to cope." And some things seem so big and existential that we cannot easily find the words or say them out loud.

I do not believe there is such a thing as an ordinary life or an average person. People are heroic, every day; but the story we carry can sometimes make us feel weak. Our day-to-day experiences, which we often hide in plain sight, sometimes scratch at our vulnerability. Our needs are often pushed to the bottom of the list as we prioritise the needs of others, or because we do not want to make a fuss. And yet we all matter, and each of us is far more important and more valuable than our story so far.

People come to work not just to pay the bills, but to be a version of themselves that reminds them of their individuality, unencumbered by what happens to them elsewhere and a place where they can flourish in their own right and in their own way. Work is a place where we should not be defined by life's labels; a place where we are accepted for who we are, but where we also hope to grow and to make our difference.

We must not only respect this possibility, but we must relish helping each other be what we need to be.

I ask you therefore to create the space at work for you to listen to the stories and experiences of your colleagues. I ask you to share your own story too. None of us can thrive at work on our own, but before anything can be made better, we need to listen to each other and to create the time and place for connection, understanding and for appreciation.

When we know a little of what each of us copes with every day, being ourselves and growing into our potential can be a shared endeavour. The workplace at its best is not a high performance, super-competitive, dog-eat-dog sport. The workplace should instead welcome the opportunity to help us be the best version of ourselves because of our stories and not in spite of them.

Equality is a noble word, and equality of opportunity is a noble and aspirational ambition. It is one that should not be reduced to a tick-in-the-box policy or a generic training session. Let's begin by honouring each individual, exploring their needs and their potential, and showing up for them on their best days and their worst.

We all carry a story. Let's carry our stories together.

In quiet praise of our inner introvert

Some of the qualities of leadership I most admire are revealed in the small knowing moments where to have noticed and to have cared come together and a small change is made. Opening a door for someone carrying bags, offering a seat to someone who needs it more, being silent so that someone can be heard – are all small acts of leadership, as well as of kindness.

By contrast, it is one of the tragedies of these more tabloid, populist times that so many political leaders in so many countries have chosen bombast, truth-shaping, epic indolence and institutional destruction as their leadership pathway. It feels like we are living through a new age of self-aggrandised, extrovert and entitled men.

This may be our fate for now, but it does not mean there isn't a place for us to make our mark in our own way. I would therefore like to share a few thoughts in praise of the inner introverted leader that sits (sometimes a little uncomfortably) within all of us.

Make tea not slogans

One of the first times I had a one-to-one with my chief executive, as a newly minted in-house lawyer, was a late afternoon briefing on a case I was managing. He called me up to his office so that I could tell him what was happening. It was getting late, and his PA was packing up. The CEO asked me if I would like a cup of tea and I hesitated because I could see the PA was about to leave. However, before I could say anything, the CEO had got up and walked towards the kitchen to put the kettle on himself. I followed and we had a great conversation surrounded by a day's worth of unwashed cups. This small act of ordinariness created a space for a more relaxed and open conversation. It humanised him and showed me that leadership is as much about putting others at their ease, as it is about grand designs and slogans.

I also liked very much that he didn't inconvenience his PA just to make me a drink. It all happened without fuss and fanfare, quietly but very impactfully.

Becoming a great follower

Sometimes the missing element in our development as a leader is that we didn't learn how to be a great follower first.

Last week someone called me to talk about how her manager was, frankly, not very good. The complaints were many and varied, but included delegating more work than seemed fair, cancelling one-to-one meetings at short notice and failing to put her forward for a promotion. All the thoughts she shared with me had some legitimate foundations, but what I could see as well, was how the negative narrative was feeding itself and every interaction was becoming a self-fulfilling slide into mutual mediocrity.

My challenge to her was "What would a great follower do now?" The conversation changed gear immediately and from a negative spiral of small moans, we created a list of meaningful, respectful, thoughtful shifts that might improve her situation, but might also help her boss to become a better manager too.

We should of course judge others slowly and with care; and we should judge ourselves kindly, but with a purpose to make things a little bit better. The quiet purposeful follower is likely to be much more of a leader than we sometimes imagine.

Practice strategic indecision

Procrastination is such a pejorative word, but often it is the greatest gift we can bestow on a problem. Obviously if the problem is someone marauding at you with a roughly hewn club and a blood curdling scream, procrastination might not be your best option. However, for the most part, this is not our typical office experience.

Most problems are not urgent, but on some days every incoming email can feel urgent. We are not algorithms; just because someone presses send, the answer cannot always be returned immediately. The world of email, WhatsApp, Slack etc, can sometimes make us feel that we are inadequately shielding from a storm of arrows on a medieval battlefield. The pressure to reply instantly, without careful thought and without choosing either tone or direction is in the end no more useful than a careering cart of chimps flinging poo at unsuspecting passers-by. The art is to honour the needs of our inner introvert by gently managing expectations because, when this is done well, the space created is where a quiet thought can mull and mature. I suspect it is also the best way to ensure we make the right decision.

As I have said many times, we are all leaders. The introvert within us may sometimes go unheard, and the introvert within us may sometimes seem to hold us back. However, as a counterpoint to the din and the hurtling pace of fast-forward change, the introvert within us might also be our best guide to being a leader who will pause to show thoughtfulness, reflection and care.

February 2022:

Admiring "opponents"

I am a left of centre, liberal-minded, social democrat. I was a Labour Party member for most of my adult life, and in the 2015 General Election I had the privilege of being the official candidate for the Labour Party in my home town of Cheltenham.

Here are just a few of the Conservative Members of Parliament that I admire.

Alex Chalk is the Solicitor General and my local MP. He is a hard-working, intelligent and empathic human being. I believe he cares deeply about the town I live in.

George Freeman is a junior minister in the current administration. He works bloody hard and brings a rigour and a passion to his brief that is admirable and impressive.

Tobias Ellwood is the Chair of the Commons Defence Committee. He speaks with calm authority and dignity. His language is temperate, but sincere.

As I started this list, I realised I could probably make it much longer. A long list of opponents that I admire. I will, of course, happily argue against their positions on specific policies, and I can criticise their voting records and even find examples when they have made me furiously frustrated with the choices they have made.

The point is that in politics, as in families, and in business and in life, we cannot thrive together if all we do is to destroy and divide. In the end, we thrive when we find the ground where we can accept, collaborate and build, for all our sakes.

In the last few years, first in the US, but now in the UK, there is an existential threat to our democratic traditions. If leaders continue to trash the infrastructure and the institutions, by debasing standards and processes and people, and even the rule of law, we risk good people walking away, so that only the amoral, the sociopathic and the self-obsessed can thrive.

Whether you voted for Brexit or to Remain, or for Conservative or Labour (or anyone else) we all need good people from all wings to stand up for our democracy. I don't hate Mr Johnson. I do not wish him any harm. But I want him to fail, not for Labour to succeed in a partisan way, but for our Parliament and our democracy to succeed.

The blank page

I love the blank page; it makes me pause.

I love that it is full of possibilities. I love that before the keys make their mark there is a moment of reflection where an idea begins. I love that words and ideas must work together to find a way to breathe life into each other. I love to see if the words land with ease and confidently stand in lines to hold up the ideas for others to see; or if they will need to be pulled around the page to find their place, jostling for room, before the ideas have their place and their voice.

I love the blank page. I love the potential for an unfolding narrative that no one else has seen before and I love the intimacy of how the blank page offers itself to be a place for a thought to rest.

However, for me, the blank page is less about writing and more about finding something valuable in the million thoughts I have each day. We all have ideas that swirl and gather, a murmuration of emotions driven by experiences and feelings. To capture a single thought and to let it rest and be seen, is so much more about discovery than about writing. It is a chance to reveal and honour that thought, to weigh its value and to respect and understand its place in my world. This is the privilege a blank page offers to me; it is an opportunity to discover something of myself, and to allow a thought to become a feeling. It is why I love the blank page.

This week, like so many weeks before, has been a clattering din of excitable noises. It is easy to get caught up in the commotion and only add to the noise. A working week is all too often peppered with phrases like "back-to-back meetings" and "sorry, I just haven't had time to prepare." Diaries that look like packed commuter carriages with no room to think or breathe as we travel through our non-stop days.

If we are not careful there is no time to stand and stare, as WH Davies invited us to do in his sumptuous poem.

What is this life if, full of care,
We have no time to stand and stare?
No time to stand beneath the boughs
And stare as long as sheep or cows:
No time to see, when woods we pass,
Where squirrels hide their nuts in grass:
No time to see, in broad daylight,
Streams full of stars, like skies at night:
No time to turn at Beauty's glance,
And watch her feet, how they can dance:
No time to wait till her mouth can
Enrich that smile her eyes began?
A poor life this if, full of care,
We have no time to stand and stare.

Isn't it glorious? I especially love "No time to wait till her mouth can enrich that smile her eyes began." What a beautiful way to reflect on something as simple as wanting to relish both the smile and where the smile began.

Our non-stop world is made for us by every relationship, interaction, word and deed. We inherit yesterday's bundled-up chaos and have to make some sense of it today. The clattering din will not subside and there is no time to let our souls catch up with our swirling minds. It is imperative therefore that we find our way to pause; to stand and stare.

A pause is to notice, for kindness and for caring's sake. A pause is a gift to ourselves of a space for a thought to rest. It is a moment to be our true selves, where we may put down the weight of the world and rest our weary cares.

As you now know, one of my pauses is the blank page, but what are yours?

When we know the pauses that work for us, it is easier to find them, trust them and to use them; and it is easier to love how they make us feel. A time set aside, made by us, for us, where the din subsides.

I spoke to someone this week who has been through a dreadfully undermining time and now needs a little help to find a new job. She is still spinning from all that has happened, but she was also anxious to begin finding her new role. She asked me how I could help her to find it; "the first thing we should do" I suggested respectfully, "is not to look for a new job, but to look for the pauses that help you to find you."

Do not conform to the pattern of this world, but be transformed by the renewing of your mind

Last week a contributor to BBC Radio 4's "thought for the day" shared a few words that stayed with me and it felt good to reflect on them for a while.

"Do not conform to the pattern of this world, but be transformed by the renewing of your mind" (Romans 12.2)

For those who have followed my blog for the last year or two, you will know that I often dwell on the role of lawyers in business and in society. You will also know that I feel things are a little broken at the moment, despite the professional rules that apply to all, and the considerable care and expertise shown by the vast majority.

Whatever brilliance we know is achieved each and every day, we know that bad stuff happens too. In recent years we have seen the Post Office scandal; examples of NDAs used to suppress whistleblowing and to protect the perpetrators of significant harm; and law firms that aggressively represent State actors or global businesses with limitless resources to fight, deflect, delay and intimidate.

It is an uncomfortable truth that good people, with good intentions and honourable track records are sometimes at the heart of situations that in hindsight look like they helped to facilitate harm.

There are wiser people than me who will say that to play hard, but within the rules, is perfectly legitimate; however, I cannot help wondering if we are grooming our younger lawyers to be brilliant tactical magicians, while failing to develop their sense of humanity and justice.

In part my worry is about the tension between powerful people and institutions, and the lawyer's duty of independence. At what point are overwhelming resources and intimidatory power a disfigurement on our sense of fairness and of what is right?

The preeminent ethical duty is not to undermine the administration of justice and in doing so to act with integrity and with independence. The role of lawyers therefore is to balance power with enough checks and controls to ensure that justice is served first. The role of lawyers is to help create the level playing field for evidence to be weighed. However, the role of lawyers is also to speak truth to power and to hold a standard well above what is merely expedient.

When a law firm acts for a global corporation or a state actor against an investigative journalist, for example, is it right to overwhelm the journalist with intimidatory and costly process?

When whistle-blowers are silenced by NDAs prepared by the legal team of a sexual predator, is the client funding lawyers to undertake reputation laundering?

When deliberately crafted words so imbalance a contractual relationship a sub-postmaster becomes liable for accounting discrepancies that are demonstrably not her fault, has the legal team set in train a means to ruin lives?

All lawyers need to reflect that the power of who pays their fees or their salary is not a "happy days" cash-cow, but perhaps a warning flag that requires them to bring their ethical A-game to all that they do.

Reiterating and upholding a meaningful sense of what independence means for lawyers today is one way to frame this need. My concern is that if we are not careful, complacency and a tendency to unthinking acceptance of our own infallible judgment, allows independence to become a passive behaviour that absolves lawyers from questioning and intervening. Provided we have advised on the risks, we can retreat to a safe distance, holding our noses and considerably richer.

I strongly believe that this is not acting with independence.

Independence is a responsibility to positively intervene when something does not feel right. It is the duty to be a critical friend, to challenge and to examine. It is having the awareness and courage to contemplate all the possible consequences of an instruction and to be prepared to give each consequence a voice.

I say this knowing how difficult it will be. No one wants to hear the "cry wolf" lawyer, or the unthinking pedant or to have the thoughtless disruption that flows from an ill-judged intervention – but it is our job to be the intelligent pause for thought.

Neither is this a veiled criticism that executive colleagues are bound to do bad things if left to their own devices; it is simply a reflection that in the swirl of ambition, strategy and operational imperatives we should surround executive talent with resources to support them so that they can shine. Recently a CEO wrote to me to challenge assumptions behind some of my thoughts, and he was right to do so. I accept that there should be appropriate disagreement and not all lawyerly challenge is fair or right. My point is only that it is an important part of our job to speak up.

It is of course also true that we will rarely see when lawyers prevent bad things from happening and challenge with courage. This work will always be off camera, and I know well the care and rigour so many bring to countless situations, but we should therefore talk about it more, celebrate it proudly and let the world know that this is how it will be.

The profession as a whole must be seen to do the right thing. The ESG movement is an opportunity to put ethical thinking at the very heart of business. It creates an expectation of action beyond the self-interested short-term drivers of easy-to-win business and the rough and tumble of corporate life. As lawyers, therefore, we might like to reflect on how we interpret our duties, and how we should act, so that words like "independence" and "integrity" are not casually tossed around like decorative scatter cushions in a gilded executive play area, but have heft and meaning for our modern age.

Do not conform to the pattern of this world, but be transformed by the renewing of your mind.

Broken ribs

One day, a long time ago, the school bell rang and within seconds the corridor was its normal state of total chaos. Kids running into each other and by each other, snatching moments of freedom as they raced to their next class; a jostling swirl of chatter and limbs. It is a noise that only schools possess when the energy of adolescence meets a gap in the timetable and an enclosed space.

I pushed by a group of lads as others pushed by me. Then, a second later, my world was literally tipped upside down. I was on the floor and being violently kicked by the boys I had just pushed by. My mistake was to have bumped into the school's most feared bully and his associates. That evening, home from a brief visit to the local hospital, I nursed two broken ribs and some dented pride.

I don't think about it very often, but occasionally it pops into my mind. I was about 13 years old and I was already six feet tall, but only about eight stones wringing wet. My grandfather used to tease me for disappearing if I turned sideways, and he often chuckled that the only reason I stayed upright was my size ten feet. Age 13 my ribs were easy to break, there was no padding like the well lagged man I am today.

I wasn't bullied very much at school, but I know it left a mark. I know for example that my confidence dips when I feel vulnerable. I know that I also carry an anxiety that makes me very circumspect around people who are arrogant and overbearing; and I cannot stand to see bullying anywhere in any shape or form.

Television, radio and newspapers last week were full of the harrowing stories of sub-postmasters speaking at the Inquiry into the Post Office scandal. I felt I needed to say something, to mark the start of the Inquiry, so on 15 February I posted a tweet that said:

> **Paul Gilbert** @LBCWiseCounsel · Feb 15
> A small part of the lawyer in me says let the Inquiry take its course, there's a time for comment and action when everything is laid out. A much bigger part of me is just ashamed. As a profession we must live up to our own rules, and promise never, ever again. #PostOfficeScandal

I used the word "ashamed" quite deliberately because I am ashamed. I am ashamed because lawyers have facilitated corporate bullying on an industrial scale. I am also ashamed because from the day I qualified on 16 February 1987 until 15 February 2022, I had never felt before that there was something fundamentally wrong with the legal profession. I know things go wrong, and I know there will always be bad apples, but I have never believed in a systemic flaw.

I am now certain, however, that there is indeed such a systemic flaw. For too long lawyers have conflated gold-plated client service, demonstrable commerciality and their own aspirational advancement, and elevated these three things to be the loadstar of high-performance professionalism. In doing so lawyers have walked passed their one true calling, to be the balance in the system that ensures the powerful cannot bully without consequences.

The Post Office, and others, have used legal process to facilitate egregious bullying when their lawyers should have been the last hope for doing the right thing. The Post Office did not break ribs, the Post Office broke lives.

As a profession we need to pause for thought. We need to get a grip of our moral compass, and we need to see that we have become part of the problem when by definition we should be part of the solution.

This is an existential moment for lawyers who for decades have been force fed on the lexicon of needing to be "business partners" of "never saying no" and "finding a creative way" to meet the client's needs. Enough. This is a reset moment.

The time has come for lawyers to reassert that their primary responsibility is to act in the best interests of justice, not their clients, and to do so with integrity and independence. It is time for lawyers to be proud that they give advice without fear or favour, and that if necessary they will challenge even their most high-profile and fee-heavy clients because doing the right thing always matters more than doing the expedient thing. It is a time for all lawyers to promise that they will never, ever facilitate bullying again.

The majority, the vast majority, of course can hold their heads high, but that is an even greater reason to reclaim what makes the legal profession precious and vital. The profession must not slide to a place where it is little more than a home for well-spoken and expensive system-gamers.

There should be no place for bullying in the school corridor; but there must never, ever be a place for bullying in our legal system.

An armada of love in small boats of hope

It is hard to write, say or do anything at the moment and not feel that it will be inadequate or trivial in the face of what we can all see, hear and read.

I also know that it is only a small step to then feeling overwhelmed by a sense of helplessness and to believing we can do nothing, say nothing or be anyone that makes a difference.

This is how bullying works, whether it is in the playground or the boardroom, whether it is in an abusive relationship with a partner who hurts us, or a country who invades us. Bullies want us to play small so that they can look big. They want us to say nothing, so that they are the only voice that can be heard. And bullies want us to be stiff with fear, so that they can move around us without challenge to do even more of what they want to do.

For a bully there is never enough, because there is never any satisfaction in having more, only in trying to get what they still do not have. Once something is within their grasp, it immediately becomes less important than what they still do not have.

The bully knows that if they exist outside of the rules that normally bind us, those same rules become weaker and at the same time they appear to tie us in knots. The bully treats our wish for normalcy, cooperation and compromise as character flaws that he is free from observing. The bully also knows that if we try to bully him back, then he was self-justified in behaving badly all along.

However, we are not helpless and anything we say or do is neither inadequate or trivial, because literally everything that ever becomes important starts improbably small and seemingly inconsequentially. The greatest love affair of your life started with a single kiss. The job of your dreams started with a hope that you might do well in an interview. Your best friend was once a stranger and the memories you now hold dearest were once just faint aspirations

Our worlds can be rocked at any moment by accident, illness, redundancy, or loneliness, or indeed a million other things that can go wrong; but we are sustained in uncertain times by love and hope. These are the two things a bully can never pull from our grasp.

I know a broken relationship is not healed with just a few soft words, and illness is not cured with kindness alone; but each soft word and thoughtful act of kindness is a step towards love and hope, and a better place. While a war is not resolved in weeks or months, and generations may have to carry its burden perhaps forever, if it is carried with love and hope this burden can also be carried to a better place.

In all the unkind noise, destruction and sadness of today, I believe that the smallest moments where we show love and hope are never inadequate or trivial because each has the potential to become the reason others can love and hope too. And if the smallest act is amplified by millions of other small acts, those who need us will soon hear us.

The bully wants us to stop loving and to give up hope; we should therefore set free the love and hope within us and let it pass to those who need it now. I know we cannot stop the war with just our thoughts and prayers, but we also know that a single spark of light will take darkness away.

We are stronger when we have the love and hope of people who care about us, and when we give our love and hope to others, then we make them stronger too. The bully is therefore doomed to fail. Our acts of kindness and care, like an armada of love in small boats of hope, will sail beyond our sight and some will reach the farthest shore to offer the encouragement and courage for others to prevail. Our smallest act may be the one to change someone's world and it is our privilege to be alive at this time to try.

I know all our thoughts are with the people of Ukraine. May they know we care.

March 2022:

Read the room, see what is needed, and be the person who tries to meet the need

The world is not totally fucked up, but as we tenuously cling to the outer edges of our planet, it is easy to allow thoughts of helplessness and despair to stand in front of our good intentions blocking our path to making a difference.

The world we live in today offers immortality (of a sort) if you can stick a lighted flare up your backside at a football stadium. A spectacle that can then be live-streamed to young men all over the world, decamped in their bedrooms sitting in rank stale boxers, snarling misogynistic obscenities across the internet.

The world we live in today also means that we can sip tea while watching another country being systematically dismantled and dismembered in front of our eyes because one flawed man has lost control of any checks on decency and is overwhelmed by a desire to inflict his dystopian vision on millions of innocent souls.

Is it any wonder that the small vulnerable child that lives within all of us might be intimidated into a hopeless silence of inaction and despair?

And yet... And yet, we also live in a world where despite all its sadness and tragedy, we can still take into our hearts those moments when we see that someone else has made their difference and is inspiring others to make their difference too. The outpouring of care, concern and action to help the people of Ukraine is thankfully a thread we can all hold onto as a way through this dreadful time. Lighting a candle with a quiet prayer, a donation, a petition, or the offer of a room for a refugee, will each leave a tiny but positive impression on others who badly need to feel our gentler touch.

And away from the unfolding tragedy of war, each of us have our own stories of people who once changed us and our circumstances for the better. It might have been a teacher, or a lecturer, a manager, colleague, or a friend or mentor. In many ways just ordinary people like us, but ordinary people who in one moment, or quietly over the course of time, allowed us to be more of our potential and helped us to grow.

More than ever now, the world needs us to be the people who can inspire others.

Can we change a life for the better by helping someone to grow and to be more of their potential? Of course we can.

My existential helplessness today is, I know, understandable, but it mustn't stop me from making my difference. For those of us who have been inspired by the past kindnesses of others, it is now our turn to pay forward. We are all ordinary and full of our own insecurities and preoccupations, but we can still be an inspiration for others. Our kindness, our care, our example, our words, our deeds, our hopes and our dreams, all matter; and each of us can say and do things that potentially land in the hearts and minds of those we meet and influence.

We do not have to change the world, but we can change someone's world.

We do not have to believe that we are an inspirational person in order to do something that feels inspirational to someone else.

This therefore is my hope; that we will read the room, see what is needed, and be the person who tries to meet the need we see. Let us at least ask what we can do to help, and let us never be worried that we need permission to have a big heart and a generous mind.

Finally, if you are in a role of significant influence because you are a partner in a professional services firm, or an executive in a large corporate, or the leader of a team, then please take this moment to reflect on the leader your clients, colleagues, communities and family want you to be at this time of all times. Please be for them the difference that your leadership empowers you to be.

Let us make our difference and help others to make their difference too.

Memories will always ache, but the pain will fade and our difference will be made

Today must still be navigated even with milk running low in the fridge, a looming meeting in the diary that fills the heart with dread and a car with an undiagnosed rattle that might be nothing, or might be more expensive to fix than the car is worth. It seems that whatever the existential crisis that is convulsing the world, we don't get a free pass on an ordinary life.

When grief strikes, one of the challenges of coping is how the world appears not to notice and carries on as if nothing has happened. Of course, friends are supportive and sympathetic, but the wider world seals us in a sound-proof pain. The shops do not close, the trains still run, the work we had before does not suddenly disappear; and yet we are in a world of hurt and upset, where every memory, smell, photo and plan is tumbled in sadness, regret and tearful, awful helplessness.

When a war, fought only a three-hour flight away, unfurls minute-by-minute in our living-rooms, and accompanies our commute, and frames the tone for our meetings, we have that same sense of emotional dislocation, because we also have all our everyday, inconsequential conversations as well. How can something so terrible be happening in my social-media timeline at the same time as I am upset that I forgot to clean my shoes?

Grief is an unwelcome and uncomfortable companion. It challenges us to carry on doing ordinary things by laying daily obstacles in our way that are awkward to confront, almost impossible to climb over and pointlessly painful at the same time. It pokes us in the chest when we at last find some time to rest; grief looms disapprovingly over our shoulder when are about to laugh, and sucks the joy from a new memory by reminding us of who is not there to remember it too. Grief is a life-long guilt trip where the pain fades but where memories will always ache.

The unimaginable world of there being a war again in Europe, or of living through a global pandemic, was only three years ago. An unimagined world no more; we now collectively grieve the loss of ordinariness for those who are suffering so much. And because it is a kind of grieving the "what now?" and the "what next?" are profoundly unfathomable things to even begin to address.

Grief does not offer answers; that's not its job. Grief does not lay out a reassuring ten-point plan back to ordinary. There are no grief-hacks.

It must therefore be part of grief that it is ok to agonise over a routine email to your boss and still have quiet tears watching the evening news. It is ok to eat the last biscuit when we know that terrified souls are huddling for warmth in basements to the sound of the thunderous destruction above their heads. Grief does not give us answers, insights or wisdom. It is a just one colossal shitshow of emotional wreckage strewn about our ordinary lives.

Tragically, our hearts are now doomed to ache for Ukraine, but right now there isn't a way to make sense of anything. Now is not the time for perspective or rational thought; so while millions are displaced and search for a place not to be frightened, it is ok to be cross that the front lawn needs mowing in early March, and that the washing machine does not spin quietly like it used to. This is also living with grief.

We all know that this is far from over, and goodness knows when it will end, but all of us who have grieved also know there will be a day again when we begin to rebuild and we will show ourselves that there is a life beyond grief. We will step forward. We will be proud for the things we achieve and not just for the things we have lost. We will make a difference that puts colour and warmth into the lives of others. We will release ourselves from grief's crippling grip and make our difference again. We will show the world that it better to be renewed by love and than to be consumed by hate.

Memories will always ache, but the pain will fade and our difference will be made.

We could be heroes

This is the story of what happened at an event on 17 and 18 March 2022 when I asked a few people to come together and reflect with me on how we might make a small difference. It was called "We could be heroes".

Just for one day, for twenty-four hours, we gathered together last week. Fourteen people who had an untold story. A story they may not have shared ordinarily, but perhaps a story that they needed to share.

We spoke at length about storytelling and the messages of change, kindness and opportunity we hoped the world might hear from people of influence. We spoke of our own concerns and vulnerabilities, and of our feelings of helplessness and of powerlessness in the face of enormous world events.

But then we made a commitment. It was a commitment to put our small stories into the world, like pebbles thrown on a pond. Pebbles to make ripples that would gently move away from us and reach places we might never see.

We did not set out to be inspirational, that would be an uncomfortable ambition for most people; and wrapping ourselves in a cloak of self-regard only keeps our own ego warm. However, to share a story is also a permission for others to hear their story reflected in the world. That is a precious thing to do. While we may not change the world with our words, our stories might help someone change their world.

Having made a commitment to tell our stories, we also resolved to tell our stories well. We therefore helped each other find the colours and the pictures and the appeal. We experimented with how to craft a message so that it lands wrapped as a gift of our experience and love, and with the hope that it will be easy to unfurl and understand.

We coached ourselves not to make our stories heavy with clichés or lost in cold, hard, colourless noises. We left behind words that were empty of empathy and corrupted by corporate life's soulless over-use. There was no need to be synthetic and tortured by finding clever vocabulary, so instead we allowed our child-like voice to show that we care, to show that we need to be cared for too, and to learn that together we have a world of opportunity in which to make our difference.

I promise you that the stories we then told each other will enrich my life forever, and they will I hope enrich the lives for all who will one day hear them too.

What did we say, we few who looked ordinary, who sounded ordinary and who came together not knowing what to say or how to say it? Well, let me tell you what brilliant and beautiful sounds were made. The following words are brief and inelegant compared to what was said in the room, but they are written with love for the people who came.

There was the story of one man's Russian-born wife and the joyous family party in Moscow when he asked for her hand in marriage. His wife now gripped with pain for Ukraine and for what her nation has become at the hands of a malevolent few.

The story of the meandering butler gently sharing advice about a career where the wanderer found joy in each and every step taken, curious only for the moment to be explored, and not for what might come next.

There was a plea from a man disillusioned with his recent career turns, but now determined to change our unkind, leaderless workplaces so they become environments for us to grow and share, not places to cower and hide.

We heard of the agony of a woman whose life had been gripped by early menopause, where her bones felt broken and her words could not be spoken as meaning slipped from her life like a balloon floating away from her once assured grasp.

There was the story of a party for a sole surviving grandparent celebrating her birthday and cherishing the love for her family now especially that it was enriched with twinkling mischief in her eye.

Then a story of another woman overcoming a debilitating condition that framed her life, to then becoming stronger than she had ever imagined and finding a power-pose to fight for a life that was meaningful and full at last.

To the story of a child who said she could not focus with her undiagnosed ADHD and to her father humbled by his daughter's strength to overcome her condition and his vulnerability that she should not carry a label for life. Both, however, now freed by her bravery and his love.

To the woman who thought she cared too much, but knew in the end that this was her super-power to be used while others caught up.

To the story of a man who as a child was regularly beaten into terrified tears by his own father, now quietly cuddling his son through illness and thereby breaking mental chains that he had carried all his life.

To the funeral of a colleague taken by cancer, whose orphaned disabled son will not now have a dad to dress him each morning. A colleague thanked in a letter from the company chairman for his dedication, but a company that did not allow him to work from home to spend more time with his son.

To a wounded pigeon trapped in a kitchen, imprisoned by an overly ambitious cat, but released to recover its freedom and its life, and perhaps a metaphor for a people fighting for their homeland and their lives not so far away.

Each story was heartfelt, kind, generous and true. Each story, heroic in the telling, and shared not to shine a light on the storyteller, but to illuminate a path for others to tread with more confidence in their story too.

We listened and we laughed and we cried. Goodness me did we cry; but we shared these stories and we made them our small, beautiful pebbles to throw onto our ponds.

The ripples will now carry our love and our hopes for others to find. We could be heroes, and not just for one day.

27 March 1962

It was a Tuesday, and the date was 27 March 1962.

The Shadows had the number-one record in the UK hit parade with "Wonderful Land" but in a maternity ward of a long since forgotten hospital in Bradford-on-Avon, things were far from wonderful. A young woman called Pamela (younger than both my daughters now) nearly lost her life, giving birth to a tiny scrap of forceps delivered humanity.

The midwife had been primed on Monday evening to break the news to Pamela's husband Brian that she was gravely ill. Pamela, having gone into labour on Friday, was exhausted and in agony with her baby seemingly unable to move into position but also pressing against her spinal column. A Caesarean Section had been mistakenly ruled out, and now there was genuine concern that both mum and baby might be lost. Brian had been sent home against his wishes, worried sick for his wife, to await news. He called early Tuesday morning from a pay phone at his work and was told that his very poorly wife was alive and so was his new born son. My first day might have been my last, but (spoiler alert) here I am.

Mum reminds me of her story every year. Last Sunday we had a cup of tea together (and a glass of champagne) and she told me the story again. She always finishes by describing how she awoke from an exhausted sleep and found that I had been taken away. She screamed for her baby fearing the worst, but I was quickly brought to her, a bit battered and bruised, but I settled quickly and wrapped my tiny fingers around one of hers. She tells me each year how she had never felt such an intense love as she did in that moment, and each year I hear her story I feel overwhelmed at how lucky I am to have someone who fought so hard for me when I was just a tiny scrap of life.

It would be easy at this point to say something empty and clichéd about human potential and being grateful for every day, but I don't want to do that. We all have our own family stories, each unique to us and special. It turns out that we are all burdened by being both uniquely wonderful while at the same time being just one of seven billion similarly wonderful souls. Is it any wonder that we are sometimes confused about our place in the world?!

However, on my sixtieth birthday (I mean, WTF, sixty!) and on this one day only, I would like to say a little about me. I promise not to do it again.

I am shy and introverted, but I always prefer being with real people rather than their social media avatars. I am sometimes accompanied by a gentle depression that mostly allows me space, but sometimes it jumps on my back and I find it hard to move. Even so, and even on darker, slower days, I consider myself to be unbelievably blessed. I do not seek attention and I never (ever) want feedback, but I love to learn. I have never delivered the perfect programme and I hope I never will, because I always need there to be something I can make even better. I am stubborn as hell about some things and ridiculously relaxed about others. I don't like change, but I don't mind uncertainty.

I also have no wish to be remembered for my work; but I hope so very much that my work will be remembered.

In my head and in my heart there is no personal legacy. I do not believe I am important in any way. However, I also believe that my work has never been more important and I have never been more determined to carry on and to relish the opportunity I have to teach, to write and to influence; and in doing so to show that there is a kinder way to lead.

If all that sounds a little contradictory, I will try to explain.

To inspire someone is not to be inspirational yourself. The person inspired is the one who must get the credit. They are the inspirational one. The joy of mentoring is helping someone find a better way for themselves, but until they have taken their first steps nothing is achieved. When those steps are taken, the achievement is theirs.

I have achieved nothing; the people I help are the achievers. However, as each person is helped I want them to reflect on their responsibility to now share their gifts and blessings with others. In doing so we create a wave of kindness that gently rolls through our work and through the years of our work. My wish therefore is to help as many people as I can; and while I do not need or seek credit for doing so, I do hope so much for the time and energy to try.

OK, that's quite enough about me, but as it is my sixtieth birthday (have I said that already?) I will test your patience a little more, because I have some reflections I would like to share. They are reflections of my working life, trying to make sense of a hotch-potch of steps forward and back; mostly failing, but always hoping.

Dear Reader,

You are a leader whether you like it or not. Leadership is not about hierarchy or titles, but about influencing people and things, it is having an opinion, stopping harmful stuff, looking after a moment in time because the moment needed you to step in. Leadership is noticing and acting. Make no mistake, you are a leader.

Being a leader is the greatest privilege of your working life and the hardest thing to get right. You will make mistakes, so the only way to navigate this journey is to be true to yourself, because when all else can fail and you feel overwhelmed, your values will hold you up and allow you to breathe.

Please tell your story so others can hear their story in your words. Be the example they need you to be. Be kind (obviously) but ask for help too. Then, when you have been helped, do not look to pay back, but always look to pay forward.

We are all leaders some of the time and all followers most of the time. However, with all the focus on leadership in books, in training and with online influencers, make sure you learn to be a brilliant follower too.

We all know that a problem is easier to spot than its solution. A solution that works is the most precious thing of all. Solutions however have to be tenaciously and strenuously dug out of the problem they are embedded within, and they are hard work to release. Let's not therefore stand by and point, but step in, muck in and help to fix things.

Please care about your fellow travellers as they accompany you on your career journey. Empathise with everyone, but do not infantilise anyone. We help no one by making them dependent on us. Lift others up so that they in turn can lift others too.

Say out loud what you need. Say out loud how you feel.

When a role does not work out, move on. Always trust your judgement even when others may not; but listen to everyone and learn from everyone.

Be gracious when something goes well. Be humble when it does not. Always stay in the moment, it is the only one we've got. Remember that not everything can be fixed or made better. Sometimes we have to let things go. We should not regret trying, but we should not let trying in vain be the only thing we can do. We must learn to fail without animosity, anger or concern for what others may think or say; they did not wear our shoes. We tried our best, and now we can move on.

It is a kindness to others if we try and fit in, but we should not bend ourselves out of shape. When something feels wrong, say that it feels wrong, but then always offer to make it feel right.

We should give our time willingly when it can be used to help someone else. Being paid to help is not important. We do not improve the value of our help when we are paid for it, and we do not devalue our help when we are not.

We must try to call out harm when we see it. It will be the most courageous thing we ever do, and it is never easy; but if we can say what we see, even just saying it out loud is sometimes enough; and every infinitesimal small difference is always worth it.

Our careers matter less than the people we help. Our difference is in the behaviours and actions of those we helped to be themselves, not in the lines on our CVs or in the prizes that carry our names.

I am sixty today (I may have mentioned it earlier) but whatever our age and experience, we have never been better prepared to make our difference and so we must always care to make it. Thank goodness for the gifts we can share; but more than ever we must learn to share them well. The best of you may be in the future, but the best of you today is still more precious and more vital.

Sixty years ago today nothing much happened, just a terribly difficult birth in a long forgotten maternity ward. Not to be forgotten however is the pain and anguish felt by Pamela and Brian, or their love and joy for their first child. Their love, sacrifice and strength to carry on, not just on 27 March 1962, but throughout their married life, will be a lifelong gift for me to honour and pay forward.

I hope we may all have the opportunity to use our time and our blessings to make our difference in the world; a world that will always be improved by our love, kindness and care.

April 2022:

My hobbyhorse is not at the races

It's easy for me to rise from my armchair residency, to climb on board my hobbyhorse of choice and pontificate.

As a mere commentator, it should also be easier for me to sound plausibly wise after the event, given that I can write with the benefit of seeing how some consequences played out. Even so, I suspect it's not such a good look to sound too clever when standing in judgement of others. I am self-aware enough to realise I might just sound like the old farmer advising the hapless tourist, hopelessly lost somewhere deep in unfamiliar countryside, and trying to find his holiday destination – "Well, if I were you, and if that's where I wanted to be, then I wouldn't be starting from here."

Is it fair therefore to be too hard on the chief executive of P&O Ferries who sacked eight hundred colleagues in order to hire new crew on lower wages? Hindsight, they say, is a wonderful thing; it is our gift to the world that flows from our mistakes. It is the gift we can share, but a gift that arrived too late for when we needed it ourselves.

The consequences of his decision to fire his workforce, played out for him in real time and with alarming speed. Perhaps it just goes to show that a decision taken in a nicely appointed boardroom with a phalanx of highly paid colleagues and advisors to support you, doesn't mean you always get things right or that you can control what happens next.

If that sounds like a cheap shot from me, especially given my armchair commentator status, I find it hard not to be cynical and disappointed at the heartlessness of the implementation of the P&O Ferries decision. However, I will venture a view that it might not be a failure of governance.

Back in my day, and it is also true today, it would be an everyday occurrence for lawyers to say to their clients, in terms, "There may be reputational consequences for the option you prefer, but if that is your informed and settled decision, you are entitled to make it." It is also the case that there are many times when the law is not clear, and it is both legitimate and sometimes necessary to test its boundaries.

The P&O Ferries decision, however, is slightly different, and it is unusual for any executive to say, "I know I am about to break the law, but hey ho, I believe it is for the best." Is it possible therefore, to find a way to be slightly more comfortable with what looks like a hopelessly misjudged decision?

To colour things as positively as I can, I believe it is possible that executives at P&O Ferries believed the company might fail without an immediate and drastic restructuring to reduce costs. Their chosen way forward to avoid this, was to sack employees and hire new crews on lower wages. While it was a known legal requirement to then consult with the Maritime Union, this was ignored because they felt it would have made no difference to their settled decision and time was of the essence.

Even in such extreme circumstances it would be very unlikely for the HR director and the legal advisors to say it was ok to break the law. Assuming they gave advice not to, the chief executive was making an informed decision and took responsibility for the consequences of the decision. If he believed speed was essential, and decisiveness was essential too, and with the whole company at risk if he did not, then he may have felt he was making the best decision he could make. Advisors advise, but executives decide.

To be a little melodramatic, if the bridge you are driving across is about to collapse, sticking to the speed limit to avoid a fine is not the way to save your life.

In the last few years, we have seen some egregious governance failures, but not every failure is a result of arrogance or ignorance, or indeed a failure of governance.

The best chief executives I have worked with never made shoot-from-the-hip decisions. They weighed in the balance and respected all contributions. They respected push-back and asked for challenge, but when it came to making the decision at their pay grade, it was their responsibility, and they knew they had to live with the consequences too.

I noticed that the P&O Ferries chief executive attended a Parliamentary Committee just a few days after the news broke. He did not hide behind lawyers' advice or reputation management consultants, or more junior colleagues. He turned up, faced up and took responsibility. I am not sure we should find this to be outrageous, even if we might fundamentally disagree with the decision and especially the way it was implemented.

I don't know this gentleman or his business. The culture at P&O Ferries might be rotten and he may be the chief executive for an awful employer, but it is also possible he felt damned if he did and damned if he didn't. If he listened and if he cared, I'll give him credit for being accountable for his decision and standing in front of his critics.

It is easy to commentate, easy to have a hot-take and easy to be on the side of the angels. I know because that's me in most things I write about. So, while I think it was a terrible decision for all who lost their jobs, and I believe P&O Ferries could and should have treated people with more dignity and respect, perhaps it is not so straightforward to see this a failure of governance.

I was once told very gently that my hobbyhorse looked great, but it wasn't in the race. And that is certainly a very fair comment indeed. My hobbyhorse therefore quietly dismounted, and my armchair residency resumed, for now.

Ambition is the shape of you

What is ambition? What is its shape and colour? What is ambition's energy force? How does it compel you?

I am fascinated by the word and how it alters our perception of success and even of our identity.

When I was training to be a lawyer, my only ambition was getting to the end of the week without being shouted at or making a mistake. I never remember thinking that becoming a partner in a law firm was a thing for me. After all, I was just a little scrote of a lawyer with an unreliable 1974 Vauxhall Viva and an overdraft that gave me sleepless nights. Partners however were other worldly beings who moved about the office on silent rails, they had vast Volvo estate cars, Labradors named after historic battles, Boden-esque children named after holiday islands and houses with implausibly long drives high on the hill.

Then when I became an in-house lawyer, things changed a little. Being surrounded by people who called themselves managers, I felt more at home with the idea that I might become a manager one day. I could supervise a bit, and report up and cascade down; it didn't seem too difficult.

To be an executive leader however, well that still felt far beyond me. I think it would be fair to say that I never felt entirely comfortable with the title and its implication that somehow what talents I had made me worthy of being set apart from other colleagues.

I have realised since that leadership is not bestowed on us by a title or hierarchy, but it is something that is within all of us. It is to be human.

We do not become leaders, we are leaders; but to fulfil our potential as leaders, we must learn to trust our feelings and then let our feelings guide our actions.

If our ambition is to acquire leadership status, I think it might feel hollow when we get there. If our ambition is to make a difference, I think our roles become rich with leadership possibilities.

I remember being at one of those very fancy conferences for lawyers somewhere implausibly swanky in Europe. I was surrounded by people who wanted to be accepted as leaders. For most people this meant being the General Counsel. If they were already a General Counsel, then they wanted to be a "Global General Counsel" working in ever larger companies. These were good people, but it felt to me that some were pursuing leadership as a collection of adornments, rather than exploring their authentic leadership potential. It felt a little thin and perhaps also excluding.

Ambition, in this way, is mostly about accepting an imposed hierarchy of importance and someone else's idea of our place in it. It is reminiscent of a sort of class war. You may be a GC, but are you a GC of a FTSE? And if it is a FTSE, is it a FTSE 100? And if it is a FTSE 100, how many countries do you operate in? Do you report to the CEO? Do you have a driver? What is the colour of your executive travel card status?

It might be important in its way, but it is not the person you are or the difference you can make. It is a potential rabbit hole of joylessness, where imagination, contribution, kindness and care might disappear and where not securing the next rung of someone else's ladder, is a sign of your failure and even shame.

This is ambition where there isn't even a pin prick of light emanating from the soulless arse of apparent success.

However, what if we reclaim the word? What if we wrestle it back from all the fast-track matrix bollocks and high-performance mythology? What if the word is not about status, or our next job title, but about our story, our difference, our growth and our fulfilment?

I hope ambition can be more than navigating an HR development plan where we move ourselves around a made-up grid using only three-letter acronyms. I hope ambition can be so much more than the grinding pursuit of linear career goals. I hope we can make ambition a rich and thoughtful exploration of how we influence, share, listen, create and make our difference.

Ambition is then the shape of you.

Packing away the moments that make up some great days

Packing away one of our LBCambridge residential events, as we did again last Tuesday evening, is a time when reflection and exhaustion compete quietly for my attention. The banners are furled away, tables and chairs are stacked in corners, and the unused writing pads and pens are packed up to reappear in a few months' time. The room quickly empties of its recharging hubbub; soon the sound of animated conversation inside the wonderful Old Hall is just a fond and gentle memory of the people we have met and who we encouraged to share their stories so that they might help each other to be both brilliant and kind.

In our separate and very busy lives, we are all passing through, everyone of us on our own untrodden paths, but for a short while all our paths cross at this place and we pause together for a few moments in time; a base camp for the mind and soul. At the start of the event we hold their hopes in our hands, but by the end they now hold our hopes in theirs.

With the room now empty of people and with the doors wide open, the space fills with the sound of a distant clattering trolley taking dirty coffee cups away, and a cool evening draught arrives with a sense of my time to go.

Before I finally close the door, I sit for a little while longer on the stage and remember the moments we made them think and pause and laugh and wonder about the opportunity they have to make their difference. We asked them to be the grown-ups in the world and to make their hopes become real, because now is the time when the career gods are shining so brightly on their talents. It will not always be this way.

In a room that is hundreds of years old we are beyond blessed to sit down with delegates who, despite what they may feel about themselves, have more than a hundred years of accumulated experience between them. In such a space we know we can be certain that there will be the answers to everything; either in the lived experiences of the people there, or in their ingenuity, creativity and intellect to explore and find them.

When it is over, a sort of melancholic peace sits on my shoulders. I am filled with hope for the wonderful contribution the delegates will make. I see their ambition and their integrity and their love for their work; but I also see the risk they may exhaust their minds and bodies on the barbed fences of misplaced priorities. Most of all I do not want them to play small when they should be bold. The legal profession is a precious but precarious barricade protecting us and our society, and on which good men and women must stand together to speak truth to power. It is however more fragile than ever, and we must never take it for granted.

As I gather up my thoughts and assemble my weary bones for the drive home, I take a last look at the space where we made moments in time seem precious and real. I know these moments are now safe in the hearts and minds of our delegates; lovingly wrapped parcels of guiding wisdom that were shaped and shared in a special place, and which are now quietly tucked away for when they will be needed most.

Packing away the moments that make up some great days, but time now to close the door and turn out the lights, until the next time.

A mentor

If I had to describe what I do, I have a few things to choose from. A lawyer (once) and sometimes now a presenter, a writer and a consultant, but if I had to land on only one word, it would be mentor.

I have said before that the proudest achievement of my professional life was on 16 February 1987. It was the day I qualified and became a Solicitor of the Supreme Court. I qualified against my expectation, against my history, and against a world that was kind in many moments, but which had created structures and pathways with built-in obstacles and obsolescence for people like me.

I think I am most proud of that day because no-one can disagree with it, or qualify it, or downplay it. I became a lawyer on that day, indisputably. I was so proud of the moment, but more than anything, I was hugely relieved. The hopes I had for myself, and the hopes of those who loved me, could now rest at last. Hope had done an awful lot of heavy lifting, but like all emotions hope can be overplayed and become exhausted.

The moment was huge, but there followed years of wondering if I belonged. Perhaps climbing a mountain is not the same as wanting to live on one. There are great memories of course, and great friendships too, but I can clearly recall looking in on myself and wondering if the achievement of becoming a lawyer should have been an ending and not a beginning.

It was increasingly uncomfortable to find that at each celebration of career progression, the quiet feeling inside of me was one of trepidation thinly supported by hollow smiles. As my journey took me further away from myself, it felt lonely and added to the sense of the imposter coming ever nearer and soon to call me out.

In 2000 the millennium bug was not in software, but inside me. It was time to pause and to stop walking further away from myself. Time, perhaps, to stop climbing mountains and to find a place I wanted to call home.

The step away from being General Counsel was neither brave nor foolhardy, I was not giving up anything I wanted to keep. I had become lost. The energy to pretend that somehow this was the time of my life, and all my ambitions were being fulfilled, was simply taking me too far away from the man I wanted to be, and it was becoming unbearable. Some mornings I could not start the car and drive to work without crying. This was not fun, and it was not me.

My new business started in the year 2000. I knew very well that it might not be the answer, but it was a lifeboat. I could rescue myself and I could pause. In 2000 I had no idea what would happen next, but the decision to step off one career and to reflect on what I needed to do for myself, has empowered my working life ever since.

I have never lost my love for the values and importance of the legal profession. I love the people I work with, and I use that word "love" very deliberately. Love means I can give myself to the people I help. It means I can do so without expectation of something in return. It makes my life less transactional and allows me to find fulfilment in kindness, in valuing vulnerability, in simple acts of care, and in ensuring that the loneliness some feel is not as all-consuming as it might otherwise be.

In the twenty-two years that have passed I have travelled the world to have the most privileged access to people at their strongest and weakest, to listen and to share. I don't have a technical definition of what I do or of what mentoring means, but I know what it feels like. It feels fulfilling.

To walk beside someone for a while, to care about them, to show them some kindness, and to help them believe that their unique gifts are all they need to make their wonderful difference in the world, is the privilege of my life.

The legal profession has never been more needed, and the people in it have never carried more responsibility to do the right thing; but size, power, and money do not guarantee that the right thing is done. Indeed, sometimes these things take us away from what is right.

We have to make our difference. We have to honour the talents, opportunities and experiences that we own. We have to be courageous too, because we are the grown-ups now. But neither must we feel overwhelmed with the weight of all that is sad, broken or unkind. The smallest first step is just as important as any grand plan. The smaller the intervention, the more compelling it becomes for us to make it. If we focus on the need in front of our eyes, the more we will see how we can make things better, and our confidence will grow to make an even bigger contribution.

I hope our difference does not just live in the clipped managerial tones of our immaculately curated biographies, but lives in the rise and fall of our heartbeat as we step into a real world that needs us more than ever. Let us therefore step into our difference, whatever it might be.

May 2022:

The long walk into ignorance

When the sun is setting on a role, and dark clouds cloak our view, what stories do we tell ourselves about the truth we thought we knew? When emperors have feet of clay and their wall-hung values become see-through, what then of bedtime stories missed on our trains from Waterloo?

If your career destination is a world of tinsel status and self-regard, it will be a long walk into ignorance, passed acts of kindness and love that you have chosen to discard. The world will spin with or without you, so let it take us where it will; we may only live this moment once, but it's still our moment to fulfil. We are the architects of our future and not the tenants of our past; may your foundations be made of kindness and may your soul direct your path.

To listen is our superpower, to make a difference is our gift; when we fill our time with moments of care, even mountains can be made to shift. The follower empowers the leader far more than we ever know; we are their energy and their momentum and the reason they can grow. In return the leader's role is not to direct or to dictate, but to help everyone of us excel and therefore to create. The leader holds the light so that you and I may shine, narrating the CV stories that will become both yours and mine.

No business is an edifice that stands without its people. The concrete, steel and marble halls may be there when we have gone, but without our human stories, there is no purpose, no value and nothing to build on. Work takes a toll on all of us, but never let it take your soul. The long walk into ignorance is a bleak and friendless path, a desperately sad black hole. Therefore, be a follower of your values and let your judgement be your guide, pour your heart into things that matter with kindness by your side.

June 2022:

The follower's tale

To follow well is an act of profound and selfless leadership.

The follower's role in the success of any organisation is often poorly appreciated and significantly misunderstood. It is never just to do the job and go home; it is never just to do the leader's bidding and get paid; and it is never to be unnoticed and just to be a good team player.

To follow well is to serve the needs of the moment, of our colleagues and to represent the best of ourselves. To follow is to endorse, to hold fast and to be loyal. It is also to guide, mentor and encourage. The servant follower is the backbone, armour and lifeblood of an organisation. The follower's contribution is not always noticed in crowded noisy airless spaces, but the follower's inspiration is real and solid, and essential to the very essence of being a team where together we achieve so much more than we can achieve alone.

We can read so much about leadership, but it is the follower we should read most about. We are all, at some level, followers and we all have this extraordinary role to play.

On a universal scale, one human's contribution is barely a pixel in the film of our world. However, we are each of us the polished pieces of glass in a mosaic, all of us part of the whole and all reflective, colourful and important. On our own we may feel small, inconsequential and (perhaps) lacking purposefulness, but the follower we become allows us to be the person who plays our part in revealing the whole picture. The picture only becomes important and valuable because we are the pieces that make it so.

I have had the privileged opportunity to observe so many wonderful teams, but I have only recently started to notice properly the role of followership and how followers let our leaders succeed.

To follow is to know you have a part to play; so play your part and play it like it really matters to you. Help others play their part too. Stay in the moment and feel what needs to be done. Support those who ask for your help, but especially offer your support to those who do not know how to ask you for your help.

Protect and promote the ambition and values of your team. Be an advocate for colleagues whose voice is not being heard. Find it in your heart to speak up for your needs and always challenge what does not feel right. Do not live with regret, but be at peace with your efforts. We cannot make things perfect, but we can make them better. We can always makes things better.

Bring your ideas forward without conditions. Listen to the ideas of others without conditions. Encourage those who lead us to listen, to pause and to reflect. Be a guide for their thoughts and let your thoughts guide them.

To be a follower like this is to know we have made our difference. Together we are the interlocking pieces that form the foundation on which our team's success is built.

The follower is needed more than we can ever imagine. The follower serves all of us. We should ensure those who follow know how valued they are, how needed they are and how much loved they are too.

Leadership is

There is never a moment when you truly know if you are ready for leadership.

There isn't an exam or an interview; and there isn't a permission you need to wait for. There is just that uncomfortable dialogue between your values, your talent and your fears debating among themselves whether it is time for you to step forward.

Then one day you will be tapped on the shoulder by the gentle touch of your potential and you will know that this is your time to make your difference.

You cannot prepare for when this will happen, but you can welcome it when it does. The privilege of leadership is that it is no respecter of titles or status; it sits lightly on your soul waiting for you step into the moment and be you.

You see, leadership is not an external construct or model or a frame, it is within you and it is the whole of you. It is your anxieties, your weaknesses, your history, your childhood, your actions over years, and your extraordinary gifts.

Leadership happens when we accept that this bundle of frailty that is us, has the capacity to make a difference, just by being ourselves and in the moment choosing to act.

Yesterday we completed the 2022 LBCambridge2 Leadership Programme. Over two residential sessions six weeks apart we worked together. Faculty and delegates wrapped in their histories and their willingness to share and grow together. I am a little exhausted, but I am also inspired by the remarkable humanity, openness and generosity of the people I met. Every one of them a remarkable leader and people who are gong to make an extraordinary contribution to their worlds of work and in the communities they live in and serve. I am so lucky to know them now.

Leadership is not about grand gestures or even power. Leadership is to hold what matters to us in our hearts, to honour these things with our words and deeds, and then to live our lives trying to make things a little better.

The people of the 2022 LBCambridge2 cohort have changed my life for the better and now they will change their worlds even more than they did before.

Leadership is the way we honour our good fortune and use the blessings of our lives. Leadership is the story of our difference. Leadership is the hope we share that by noticing we can make things better.

The seventy-five-year career

As I left school in 1980, aged eighteen and headed off to study law, I had a vague notion of what a career might mean, but no idea about what retirement might mean.

If you had pressed me, I might have thought that retiring in my fifties would be about right, with a decent chance to enjoy travel and grandchildren before my hips and my mind gave up. Then, my idea of retirement would not have been based on the idea of financial security, but more about my expected lifespan and wanting to enjoy my time while I still had some energy left.

Here I am now, sixty years old and hoping that my world of work, my career, will help sustain my mind, body and soul for at least the next two decades.

If you are a twenty-something entering the world of work this year, and if you have been lucky enough to live in the prosperous West with the full benefit of education and health care, then your life expectancy will be approaching one hundred years old, and you will probably work for the next sixty years.

Children aged five this year and in their first formal year of schooling, may have a seventy-five-year career to look forward to.

This thought alone should make us want to question the whole idea of what a career means. It can no longer be a twenty-five-year trolley dash funnelling us along the same structured aisles of forced progression until we reach the checkout, like factory farmed middle-aged, middle-class sheep, burnt out, disillusioned and wandering what it has all been about.

Things are changing. We are at the start of something that will only become more pronounced and more important. As we transition to a working life that for our grandchildren might be up to seventy-five years long, I believe five ideas will guide them, and we are starting to see these ideas emerge now.

The first is that communities and networks will matter more to us than buildings or brands. The people we help and the people who help us are our most precious investment. If we commit to a purpose that is about our values, our integrity and our ability to join with people to make a difference, we will go far beyond paper thin promises that we stick on our walls, and release ourselves from the chains of HR sponsored spreadsheet progression and become people again.

Second, is that we will get even better at valuing everyone and everything at every stage of our lives. Our stories matter to the world, but first they must matter to us. CVs are for algorithms, but your story is for you, your family, your community and your legacy – we must learn to tell them well. Age, menopause, gender, race and disability will become irrelevant. In a twenty-five-year career, if you do not fit, you are lost, but in a seventy-five-year career we cannot leave anyone behind; we will all count and there will be a space and role for all of us.

Third, we must learn to celebrate what we can do, and not punish what we cannot do. We must focus on our strengths not our weaknesses. We spend far too long on our weaknesses for a marginal, temporary and too often miserable gain. Let us ask of others what they can do and ask of them to be brilliant at those things. Our world does not divide between people who are strong at everything or weak at everything; it is a false and hopeless paradigm to force ourselves into bell-curves of incompetence.

Fourth and fundamentally we are becoming increasingly aware that whatever job we have, we are just passing through. In any role we are simply working in temporary coalitions where purpose and fulfilment should matter more than status and formulaic career progression. In a seventy-five-year career we will learn that leadership and followership will be passed around and interchanged according to the strengths, experience and expertise in the group. Groups will harness our opportunity to make our difference, or we will leave. We will learn that a supportive culture where integrity, truth, consistency and fairness are important, is always going to be a kinder and more fulfilling place to work than somewhere that makes us run with the bulls whatever short-term rush of adrenalin there may be.

Finally, leaders and leadership will not be about providing artificial objectives and disconnected financial incentives; it will be about offering learning, growth, purpose and fairness. We will gravitate to kinder places. A career will be multiple and sometimes simultaneous roles, some paid, some voluntary, creating a narrative of life-long learning, where people are valued for what they can do and where the value of a team is achieved through appreciating each and every contribution.

Primary school teachers today are glimpsing the future of the world of work in the minds of the children they are starting to shape; while those of us at the far end of our working lives are digging the trenches for the foundations of their extraordinary careers to come.

The hurtling blur

When our train rattles though towns and countryside we can sometimes glimpse the world through the fences and trees that mark the line of the track. Fractions of reality, gone before we can process them properly and flying past us in rapid succession. In the hurtling blur of our onward journey there is no possibility to go back and examine the view properly, we only have that moment of snatched clarity.

And so, as we glimpse the real world beyond the hurtling blur of our working lives, we must do more than snatch moments of clarity through the dusty windows of our ever faster career trains.

The information technology revolution was sold to us as a liberation and as an empowerment. In part it signalled the democratisation of information and insight, placing the knowledge of the world and our connectivity to it, literally at our fingertips. We were no longer tied to Victorian workplace ideologies; everything would be about working smarter, not harder.

Technology however gave us the illusion of freedom, but the reality of an insatiable demand for unending digital tasks, constantly fired at us in emails and meeting requests by a world that forgot we had a life beyond spreadsheets and instant messenger alerts.

In such a world, where is our time to stand and stare? Where is our time to be free from the synthetic blur of work? Where is the time for us to tie our human feelings around real experiences so that they become the gift-wrapped ribbons around treasured memories?

Beyond the technological revolution, we are now settling into our still new hybrid realms. Our lives not only run by technology, but also fully integrated and infiltrated into our safest of safe places, our homes. Each day our online diaries enclose us in their coloured walls of commitments; our calendar prisons.

The answer, apparently, is to talk of boundaries, but what weight, heft and power does the word "boundary" have in such a world? I think not much. These boundaries are sandcastles against the incoming tide. There is no meaning to the word if it only marks the vanishing line between being overwhelmed with duties and commitments, and being too tired to enjoy our lives beyond objectives and meetings. It is the same frustration I sometimes feel when we talk of corporate wellbeing policies as if we are building mindfulness field-hospitals to patch up our injured, when we should be trying to stop the war.

We must do more than drop a word like "boundaries" into well-meaning conversations, we need to change the way we are expected to work; and leadership, as always, is the key.

In a hybrid, ever-connected, always on world, leadership has to be more than being sympathetic to such intrusions. We have to do so much more than a polite request not to send emails outside "office hours." We have to do more than offer an extra day's holiday in lieu of untold hours of lost time answering pointless messages in the middle of a holiday and across every single weekend. We have to do more, because otherwise we all turn a blind eye to the fact that our technology and working-from-home revolutions risk pouring concrete on family life.

Kindly intended words about boundaries are NOT enough. It is not the boundaries that help us, instead it is having the energy to step into a world on the other side where there is renewal, hope, kindness and fun. A place where love builds us back up and where memories are wrapped in the ribbons of the feelings that bring us joy and fulfilment.

The ever faster digital career train is not offering us a life of meaning if it hardly slows down enough for us to be in the real work outside.

Leadership must be intentional about the fair allocation of work, and provide the resources and the time to be successful. Leadership, frankly, should start by honouring the fine and fair words in each employee's contract of employment. Leadership should conspicuously respect family life. Leadership creates the space beyond work for a real life to be enjoyed. Leadership therefore helps colleagues to live, and not just to work. Leadership is stopping the train so that we can get off and properly take in the view.

July 2022:

For the pixels

This blog will not be for everyone. There is mention of poo, some swearing and my usual relentless oversimplification; one to swerve if you would prefer a quieter few minutes.

It has not been a good week for optimism has it? In this week's cavalcade of crap:

- Polio has been detected in London.
- Deborah James, a beautiful soul and an extraordinary campaigning woman, has died far too young with bowel cancer.
- A shopping centre in Ukraine was mercilessly attacked with Russian missiles,
- And the US Supreme Court overturned an historic and settled ruling with consequences that have reverberated around the world.

The litany of sadness, misery and missed opportunity is therefore longer this week than a week ago. If you are keeping score, in our head-long hand-cart race to hell, pessimism has gained a seemingly unassailable advantage.

But that's not how life works and that's not the whole narrative of our days. We do not live by the editorial decisions of TV news channels. Our individual happiness is not an algorithm of all the good things and all the terrible things to create a sort of misery coefficient app. The TV news may appear to be a highlights-show of the best terrible things this week, but there is no league table at the end. We are not relegated because Huw Edwards frowned deeply at the camera last night.

I am not saying we should be unaffected by these things, clearly we are deeply affected, but neither must we be manipulated.

In our rush to make sense of terrible things we inevitably want answers, but in wanting answers we are also guilty of wanting simple, unchallenging truths. We seem increasingly to live in a binary world, where we talk of us and them. I think we do so because we are overloaded with information, so we try to simplify things. We want debates to delineate neatly into "for" or "against". We try to reduce the most complex and unfathomable situations that have evolved over decades (even centuries) to a few column inches. An hour-long documentary is presented as an in-depth study.

But that is not how life is, is it? What has happened to you in just the last hour would take a lifetime to explain to a stranger. So, let's not trade headlines and hot-takes on twitter as if they offer a reliable rounded view.

This blog is guilty of the same thing. Some of you will agree, some of you will disagree. That's because I am both a little bit right and a little bit wrong. However, when we are dealing in sadness and misery, we should be careful not to act like we are a consumer at an "all you can eat" buffet.

Time to give our heads a wobble.

I was once asked to help a team devise their mission statement. They wanted to be a "world class" this or that. They weren't. I suggested instead, "We will try not to fuck things up too much or too often."

I'd like to suggest that this should be the only mission statement any company will ever need. It is also the only truthful political manifesto, and the only personal objective in any development plan that we should aspire to.

We are here, for now. We are infinitesimally small. We are not even a pixel in the feature film of our planet. Time then to worry about things that only a pixel should worry about. It's not about what happens, but it is about how we behave. That's the one thing we can influence. Life may be fortuitous or capricious, but how we behave can be certain.

Polio has been detected in London. Thank goodness for science. Thank goodness for the means to find out and control it again. Meanwhile you and I can still be kind and loving people.

Deborah James lit up the world. We also now know that we must absolutely check our poo. Please check your poo. While checking our poo we can still be kind and loving people.

The missiles are a devastating reminder that any war is a tragedy wherever it rears its ugly head. We are all diminished when life and livelihoods are taken violently, but there are seven billion of us and only one small troubled white guy in the Kremlin. Our collective mark will be more indelible than his, and therefore even more reason to be kind and loving people to prove it.

The US Supreme Court decision on abortion rights is a reflection of a world divided. Also, a timely jolt that we need to be collectively and constantly vigilant to protect the rights fought for by generations before us. Complacency is the enemy of our freedoms far more than any politician or judge. Today, I cannot change the US Supreme Court decision, but I can support and fight for those who need to feel supported at this time. We can be kind and loving people and still fight like hell for what we believe in.

Bad stuff has always happened in this world. Some events will take the energy from our souls and sadness can envelop any of us at any time. We are all vulnerable and everything we have won is only held if we work together. For everyone's sake a little more kindness and love will not make anything worse and may just make some things a whole lot better.

This blog hasn't been written by Pollyanna. I am inadequate, sometimes lost, often wrong, and always weak, privileged and guilty; but I have a capacity to love and to be kind. I also know, more than ever, that we must never passively submit. We should be angry. It is important to shout at the world sometimes and loudly exclaim "FOR FUCK'S SAKE, WHAT NOW?!

I cannot control much, and I can influence very little on my own, but I am not helpless and I am not without hope. I promise I will try not to fuck things up too much or too often.

You and I may only be pixels in this mad world, but we are beyond measure precious pixels for all that. Even more reason therefore to check our poo. Please take care.

About a blog

I am sometimes asked how I go about writing my blog.

I usually start writing it on the Wednesday or Thursday before I post the blog on Sunday morning. Typically, I have two or three thoughts that I would like to develop. These thoughts are never grand or inspirational, clever or wise; indeed, they are often very mundane. This week for example I have been pondering two blog thoughts; the first was whether a handwritten "thank you" note would be nicer to send than an equally heartfelt but more immediate email after someone was so wonderfully kind to me; the second thought was to wonder how much time is too much time to sit in front of my laptop before a video call is due to start?

As you can see, this ain't no revelatory rocket science, but once the idea feels like it might have something to say, then I need a way into writing the blog itself.

I know I must have all the words I will need, but knowing a few hundred words is a bit like owning house bricks without necessarily knowing how to build a home. My way in, is to find the metaphorical door on the idea, because this is the place where the idea starts to come alive as a blog. The door is often a personal reflection that allows me to set a context for the idea. The idea is now an honoured guest to be welcomed into my mind, made to feel at home and offered a comfortable place to sit.

From the initial bare idea to putting the words on a page will take be no more than hour. I write as I speak, and I find myself having a conversation with the idea. Where are the edges of the idea? Where is the meaning I want to uncover? What does the idea want to say?

Then, when this is done, it is time to leave the words alone to gently settle. The blog now has its own existence, but it has not yet found how to stand on its own, so I leave the blog alone for a while because when I return to see how it is getting on, I am confident it will find a way to speak to me in a fuller, rounder and more thoughtful way.

Saturday tends to be the day I return to the blog. My job now is not to rewrite or change too much, but just to bring the messages into focus and to let the colour in the words have their time to shine. My writing is now less about the idea and much more about how the idea can flourish. It is a little like composing a picture and I try to place the idea so that it looks its best. Words become the cushions that support the idea, and the words are the way the idea is lit and the frame we place the idea in. I want the words to let the idea feel relaxed and comfortable for others to see it at its best.

On Saturday evening I load the blog to our website, and then on Sunday morning I read it one more time before I press the publish button. I read it now as you are reading it. It feels like the first time I have seen it and somehow not something I have created. It exits now because the idea wanted to be heard and I had the privilege of giving it a little space.

Of all the blessings in my life, writing is the surest way I have to settle my swirling mind. The dialogue with an idea is a kind of meditation and something I suspect I will always do whether published or not.

The final act of writing any blog is allow it to end gently and to respect the reader's time.

We are sometimes asked to think big, especially in work. People at an interview will ask us "what is your big idea?" We are encouraged to be innovative and to be comfortable with transformation. However, my blog is about honouring our smallest ideas and giving then a place to be loved and seen. We all know that mountains are a magnificent and monumental landscape, but we also know that the pebbles on a beach offer infinite variety and beauty at our fingertips. Imagine if the thousands of thoughts you have each day are the pebbles on the walk of your life; shouldn't we make time, sometimes, to pause and to look at them closely? There is such beauty and meaning to notice in each and every one.

The great bacon roll debacle

I had the great pleasure to be at Lord's last week. It was a lovely treat. A place where the gentle hubbub of a contented crowd might just be the most blissful sound a herd of grazing humans can make. It is the sound of thousands of conversations that nestle in the weft of the unfolding narrative of a cricket match. It is partly the sound of relaxed good fortune and partly the sound of people finding joy in the lost art of being distracted together. On a warm summer's day that rolls gently into a sun-blessed evening, it would be hard for me to find a better definition of living my most perfect life.

However, last week something unexpected happened. Lord's made the quite extraordinary and unfathomable decision not to sell hot bacon rolls before the match began. Apparently, the 1pm start for the game meant there were no bacon rolls for the ludicrous rationale that bacon rolls are a breakfast food, and this was lunchtime.

Regular readers of my blog will know that I am a consistent advocate of working with whatever fate lobs in our direction. I believe we can learn from the exponents of theatrical improv and that an unexpected change of direction is therefore a gift and not an obstacle. I also mentor people to count their blessings in the midst of swirling uncertainty and to trust their judgement as their superpower. However, on this occasion I reacted as if I had been slapped by a stranger. I muttered for some minutes under my breath. FFS Lord's, you just cannot make unilateral decisions of this magnitude and not expect some shit to be lost.

As I slept on my thoughts, however, I reached a point of understanding that I might not have found without the bacon roll catastrophe.

I realise, of course, that the absence of bacon rolls is not the end of the world, or even likely to spoil an afternoon at the cricket; but neither is it entirely trivial. While I am self-aware enough (just about) not to bang on like Major-General Tufton-Bufton hankering after matron's eggy soldiers, changing traditions is never a small change.

Traditions and customs sit deep inside our identity. A change for some people might seem inconsequential; but the exact same change for some other people, might undermine their very sense of who they are. Change might seem small, but we should be mindful from whose perspective we are looking.

I know (of course, I know) that I am stuck in my ways. It's not just bacon rolls. I like my event tickets to be things that are printed on substantial paper and to fit my wallet; tickets should be a keepsake of a magical memory, not just a means of entry. I also love my dear old Nokia phone because the battery lasts 3 months and it protects me from 24/7 connectivity. And a bacon roll before a cricket match connects me to the joy of the little boy inside who still cannot believe how lucky he is to walk into Lord's to watch the game he loves.

Therefore, if you make me have an electronic ticket-app-hoojamaflip, or tell me I must have a smart phone or change my decades long routine at a cricket match, you do not update me, you lessen me.

The next time I hear myself suggest to anyone that small change is an opportunity, I will remind myself that the absence of a mere bacon roll resulted in me having a near existential crisis while composing in my head a whole series of unsent letters to the chief executive of the England and Wales Cricket Board.

Of course, change may be necessary, appropriate and well-intended, but we should also think about what the change represents and not just what the change is. Becoming the rounded leader certainly means becoming efficient at implementation and clever at strategy, but it also means knowing that compassion is an essential requirement, even for apparently inconsequential change. The Great Bacon Roll Debacle (as it will now be known) is my new benchmark for how we need to take care of anyone on whom we impose our view of small change.

And if anyone from Lord's reads this piece, please remember that it is because people care that we are blessed to love the time we share.

How much does an email weigh?

Before Tim Berners-Lee said "This is for everyone" there were no emails, no internet and no Wi-Fi. The only hot spot was on my chin, usually after a cheap chocolate binge. Now, in 2022, we know that our digital world pervades and invades everything. It is a saviour, a provocateur, an assailant and an inspiration. But does digital weigh anything? Do all those trillions of terabytes stored on servers and fired between devices, swirling and swarming around our heads every second of every day, have a mass? Or a smell? Or a colour? If digital exists, what is it made from?

It has been an uncomfortable week. Some sad and difficult days for my family.

I ask these questions therefore not for the answers, but for the distraction. To let you know that I need a distraction.

Sometimes we need to be distracted by nonsense. Sometimes we need the safety of thinking about something small and inconsequential to help us live in a world of overwhelming uncertainties and undermining fears. Sometimes issues and concerns are so big that we need the distraction of something small to anchor us in a moment in time. We need to know that we can still find some things reassuringly ordinary.

I remember as a small boy watching the TV news with my grandmother one day. There was a terrible famine in East Africa and the pictures were of searing scenes of poverty, hunger and helpless distress. These appalling terrors were played out in front of us as we ate our plentiful tea off trays on our laps. As the news programme ended and we moved on to the weather forecast, my nan said to me quietly that she didn't think the newsreader's tie was very nice.

Many, many years later, I joined a company in the North West of England. My personal life was in a very unhappy place and the company I joined within six months of me starting had begun talks with a rival to take us over. At the time I had not yet relocated and I was living out of a suitcase in pokey hotels. I was disconnected from everything that was familiar and especially from family and friends. My career (such as it was) was fading into nothing. I literally could not think about the future because everything seemed to be a dark dead-end. However, I had a battered old tape-cassette player and I would play Born to Run over and over and over again. I would shout out the lyrics as if they were mine. Even now, a lifetime later, when I hear the opening drum roll play, for a second, I am lost to memories that hurt like hell, but within a song that anchored me until the darkness began to lift, slowly revealing the countless new blessings of my subsequent life.

Some things are just too big to solve quickly. Some things will hurt forever. We know there isn't a formula for success, or a life manual. Sometimes we just need to find a way to get through the day. If that means finding distraction in the inconsequential, so be it. If we can smile at nonsense, be irritated by the banal, pause on the obtuse, or belt out a song, then in that moment we are not consumed by the storm.

These moments do not solve anything, but they are tiny little threads to tie us into normality and which hold us in place. When the waves crash over us, our only purpose is not to be swept away.

When my dear old nan noticed the newsreader's tie, I know she wasn't being heartless, she just wanted to protect me from something truly horrific.

When I ponder what an email weighs, I know no-one cares, but it takes me to a moment that is away from all the noise around me. And when the Boss starts to sing, I know I will be fine...

...'Cause tramps like us, baby, we were born to run.

Please therefore love your distractions and hold them close. Love the little absurdities of our lives, and love our ability to be lost in a moment when our days are long and sad.

And please take the greatest care of yourselves because, whatever an email weighs, you are precious beyond measure.

August 2022:

A quiet reflection on love and gratitude

I was just a few minutes old when mum put her finger in the palm of my tiny hand and I closed my fingers around it. Love can be revealed in so many ways, but those few seconds stayed with my mum for her whole life. For as long as I can remember, on every one of my birthdays since, she has told me about that moment.

Sixty years later and just a few days ago, she lay peacefully in her bed at home, with the end nearly upon us. I put my finger in the palm of her hand and she closed her fingers around mine. I have known all my life what it has meant to be loved by her and in that moment she told me again for one last time. At a time of unimaginable pain, I will always be grateful for those few seconds.

Throughout the last three days of mum's life we (that is my brother, sister and I) were with her. We sat with mum, chatted about old memories, and reassured her that we would look after each other. My brother Jon and sister Poppy are very special souls indeed who are inspirational people in my life. I could not be more grateful for their love, support and example. One day I will write about them properly because their life stories are truly extraordinary. While we have always lived our lives in different worlds, when we are together we are very obviously our parents' children – held, balanced and renewed by the gifts mum and dad left within us.

They showed us how to be kind, and to care about what we do and the people we are with, and they lived everyday being grateful for their blessings. Above all they showed us that by loving each other, we will always have a soft landing whenever we fall. For these things and so much more, I will be forever grateful.

A life lived in gratitude however is not a life without hardship, or worry, or loss. I have been thinking a lot about gratitude in the last few days. The pain and sadness I feel now is not reduced by being grateful for all the many blessings in my life. To be flippant for a moment, if you stub your toe on the leg of your bed, it does not matter how fine your bed is, it is still going to hurt like hell.

However, I now see more than ever that my gratitude is far more than being socially polite or a learned modesty to my good fortune. It is my lifeboat as I am tossed around in this boiling ocean of grief. Gratitude is what I am hanging onto for the peace it offers away from the overwhelming din of sadness. It is also the calming touch of mum's love, and the love of so many people around me, and knowing I am lucky enough to carry this with me forever, whatever I must face or endure.

Gratitude is not an answer to pain, but in the depths of the sadness I feel today, I know it is my path back into a world of love, hope and caring. A world where I will try to live up to the gifts and blessings of my life and to be grateful for the love of wonderful people.

Mum, thank you for everything; please take care. My love and gratitude always.

September 2022:

Together again

Earlier this week I spent a few late summer days in Budapest. The sun offered September warmth that meant the shady side of the street was not quite warm enough, but the sunny side was a little too much. The Danube looked still and peaceful, as if composing itself to be photographed, and the historic Parliament building played with light and shadow, looking every inch the carved marble edifice in a fantasy blockbuster film.

I was in Budapest to work with a client to discuss and encourage thoughts about their roles as future facing lawyers for a global institution. I have not been overseas since February 2020 and a lot has changed in the world since then. I left the UK feeling a little lost and out of my depth; anxious about navigating an airport as if it were my first time, and anxious about speaking to a group of clever young people, wondering if the words I might say would make any sense to anyone anymore. I also wanted to phone my mum to tell her that I was ok, so that she could tell me that I really was ok.

The client was delightful. Every single colleague greeting their friends, old and new, with warmth and appreciation and making me feel welcome and involved as well. The days flew by, and as I flew home, I knew something important had happened for me about feelings of loss.

Loss of anything that matters, whether a parent, or the connection with our place in the world, or our sense of role and contribution, even the loss of a much-loved Monarch, is not easily explained, rationalised or coped with. What is seemingly existential is felt viscerally and personally. The enormity of loss becoming jagged edges of pain and of aching relentless unease. We cannot intellectualise loss; but we can certainly feel it.

Before I spoke to the group, I had walked along some of Budapest's attractive, but careworn streets, evocative of quiet corners of Paris. As I walked it was hard not to have a somewhat surreal internal dialogue with myself about "what on earth am I doing here?" This felt different from my more familiar imposter syndrome, and felt more like a quiet contemplative befuddlement of purpose and role and direction.

Back in the meeting room it was my turn to speak; my turn to try and engage the attention of lawyers who had centuries of experience between them. I spoke of feelings, of noticing, leading, changing and of caring. And I spoke of kindness, of loss and of finding peace in the stability of the foundations that we can build with each other and for each other. I don't think I could have said my words in an online world. I could only have said them in a room where eyes widened with resonance and our shared vulnerability could be felt and not just described.

We have lost so much in so many ways, but when we are together again, properly together, we become more than our worries and so much more than our fears. We can also more easily gather around us the hope that we need for our futures.

May our troubles today and the loss we feel today, encourage us to find solace in the company of friends, family and colleagues; and may we also find hope in the warmth of what we can share with each other and build for tomorrow. May our purpose be to spend time together.

Gifts that tell your story

It is the time of year when I typically post a cheery picture of Queens' College, Cambridge and mention that once again it is my good fortune to be back for our bi-annual LBCambridge programme. Sadly, not this time and the 30th iteration of the event will have to wait.

In September 2006 we ran the event for the first time. It was a bit clunky and some edges needed knocking off, but we knew it was going to be ok.

I often talk about the pleasure of working with the delegates and our faculty, and the joy of having our wise owls sharing experiences and wisdom so generously. I sometimes comment on the dedication and commitment of my team who, from the date a delegate registers to long after the event is over, look after and encourage every individual as if they were the most important delegate ever to come. However, I don't often talk about how I feel about the event and what it means to me.

If you know me, you will know that I do not relish my role as a presenter. I feel the weight of responsibility to give the very best presentation I can, and it feels almost overwhelming to have so much trust placed on the things I might say. But I also know that if I share well, I show everyone that to give of our best is to honour the time we share in the company of others.

If you know me even a little bit, you will also know that I am not good with feedback. I pour my heart and soul into the work I do, and I feel incredibly vulnerable as a result. I am not arrogant enough to think I couldn't be better or that we need to constantly evolve what we do, but

I don't want to hear feedback at the point I feel I have given everything and there is nothing more I can do.

I am conscious therefore of not always sounding like I love what the event has given me. If all you see is the scared presenter or the guy avoiding feedback, it is possible that you might miss how lucky I feel to be in the room at 7pm on Sunday evening, when my microphone is tuned up and I can say, "good evening and welcome".

Despite what our website says, the event is not really about training skills or giving delegates tools or even about sharing experiences. We do all these things and we do them thoughtfully and well, but this is not what the event is about. The event is about creating moments for delegates where they may realise that the gifts they have are more extraordinary than they knew and are theirs to use. Gifts that will benefit their families and communities, as well as their colleagues and businesses. Gifts which can shape the world they influence; gifts that are to relish and explore.

We are not passengers in our life stories; we are the leading players and the reason there is a story at all. So let's make sure we narrate a story where we use our gifts well.

When I stand on our stage on the Sunday evening at the start of every event, my heart is racing and my mind is almost blank with fear, so there has to be a compelling reason for me to be there. That reason is the hope we will loosen the ties on our potential so that we may shine our light in a sometimes darkening world. This feeling may not happen for everyone who comes, of course, but it is my hope.

Can you imagine the pride I have even knowing that this is a possibility and the overwhelming sense of joy I feel when delegates, sometimes years later, mention to me what the programme has meant to them?

Last week we took the hardest decision of all to cancel September's event, but it was undoubtedly the right call. We wanted to respect our delegates' conflicting needs and not to impose our selfish requirements on our caterers, cleaners, technicians and all the many behind-the-scenes contributors. We knew we could not go ahead and still deliver what the event is about. After losing events through Covid lockdowns, this is a big blow for us, but the sadness is not in lost revenue, it is in the lost opportunity to help others see in themselves what I know is waiting to be uncovered.

If I am honest, I am a little lost right now. I am still grieving for my mum, and I think I needed the event to give me a time with a different focus. As I have always found, there is no better way to recover from loss than to give the best of ourselves to others. I firmly believe that when love and kindness are shared it is always repaid somewhere else where it is needed even more.

So, until we can meet at LBCambridge again, and we will, please take care.

October 2022:

What matters...

Life events challenge settled thinking. It is a cliché I know, but then that only serves to prove the point rather than to undermine it.

I am not now going to write about seizing the day, or encouraging anyone to tell their boss what they really think, or resigning to swim with dolphins. If these things float your boat, go fill your boots. However, my clichéd challenge to my settled thinking is a little more unnoticed than these things.

One of the joys of my work is the freedom to explore potential. I am not always sure how it happens, but I believe we create a quiet pause for people to hear their own thoughts. This is the start of understanding what we might need in order to succeed at being ourselves. I am very lucky to be in the room with people when they see that their potential is something that they can truly own.

However, for the last little while I have been worried about whether this is enough. I am not too sure how much longer I will be able to persuade people to take a chance on discovering something important about themselves, or whether the dash for rolling out formulas, frames, models and modules will mean we slip away from company budgets and your curiosity to know how we can all make our difference.

In the last few weeks I have wondered if it really mattered. Was I still doing it because it was what I have always done and what others expected of me? Or was I doing it because it still mattered? I apologise if this sounds a little self-indulgent. It is self-indulgent, but I want to share this thought because I suspect that sometimes we all wonder whether what we do really matters.

So, spoiler alert... It matters, but it is the way we do something, not the thing itself, that matters the most.

The space we allow others to occupy, and the words we respect even when we disagree with them, and the love we give to the people in our world and to their ideas, allows that love to live on even when we move on.

My reflection is that what we do to make a living matters less (this is just a contractual arrangement of which there will be many) but what we do to make living worthwhile is everything.

Recent life events have challenged my settled thinking. My settled thinking had become a little lost in an equation of effort and output, when it should have been nothing of the sort.

My job is not to monetise your potential. It is to let your ideas roll and to trust they will find places to rest. Ideas should roll without any commercial ambition, and be allowed to either thrive or to gently fall when the energy in them has gone.

My job is not to be the perfect font of guidance, but to have the courage to make a new mistake every day and to accept how vulnerable this may make me feel. Wisdom does not come from certainty, but from vulnerability.

My job is to make others feel that what they do matters.

The existential loss of a familiar routine through the pandemic, or the loss of a guiding north star, or the grinding rebuilding of a business when things do not go to plan, are all life events that challenge settled thinking.

I do not welcome the loss, which I know will remain raw and profoundly sad for some time to come. I also wish it were easier to rebuild a business held back by so much disruption; but thank goodness for the challenge to settled thinking and the opportunity to remind myself of really matters to me.

From Baker Street to Moorgate, a needle pulling thread

Like a needle pulling thread, our work with its joys, frustrations and some sadness will reveal a picture of our endeavours. A tapestry over time of effort, anxiety, pride and likely occasional disappointment. Each CV a steppingstone path mapping the hindsight of our choices and (hopefully) our triumphs.

Every career starts as a story to be told; the archetypical tale of tyros and magic beans, of dragons and daring do, that one day will tell of how we became the all-conquering super heroes and masters of the universe.

And yet, I so firmly believe that the relentless pursuit of a destination story is going to be flawed. It is never where we aim to be that matters nearly as much as how we travel in the moments, months and years before we arrive.

Most weeks I am in London for at least one day, and one of my familiar Underground tube journeys is from Baker Street to Moorgate on the Hammersmith and City Line. A newer train with open carriages and weak but still welcome air-conditioning. Passengers, young and old, quietly nodding within their AirPod worlds, or earnestly focused on a book, or staring stoically ahead waiting for their stop. Each person is an extraordinary story. A birth, a country of origin, a life with or without families, adventures, relationships, memories, hopes and fears. Each with a future that they want to shape, to be the architects of their destiny and not the tenants of their past.

Each carriage is a kaleidoscope of shapes and colours, and all of us are gently shaken into one unique pattern of people as we pass through stations until it is our turn to step from the train and into London's overground world. I sometimes long to know their stories. Where have these people been, what have they seen, what do they feel?

Being so close to their stories, but knowing I will never hear them, intrigues me and amuses me and is, in its way, my meditative pause between my meetings above ground. It is also the microcosm of my concern about our careers. It does not really matter if we get off at Great Portland Street, or Euston Square or Farringdon; but what did we learn from the stories of our fellow passengers?

Did we learn? Did we share? Did we grow, because between us we will know so much more together than we will ever experience on our own. Our careers should not become a silent ride to Moorgate where all we do is count the stations towards our destination in studied avoidance of the all riches around us. Instead, may our careers become the gently shaken kaleidoscope of what we can learn and apply in the times we share to make all our journeys richer, fuller, and more memorable.

Please do have a destination in mind and, by all means, know when and how you want to get there; but love the company of those who share our journeys too. Your CV will become the map of your Underground tube line; but let your heart be full of the stories between the stops, like a needle pulling thread, a tapestry over time, telling your story in the colours of all who we meet along the way.

Leadership ain't easy, but...

Overtly political blogs are not always a joy. I sometimes stray into this area and it is a mixed blessing for me and I suspect for those who read my words; so, please give this one a miss if you have had enough of the news and endless commentary. I am not saying anything you don't already know.

If you have decided to read on, this won't be too ranty or polemic, and I hope not offensive either. Also, safe in the knowledge our Prime Minister will never read this, I do not feel I am adding to the burdens she carries, but it does feel she is in a bit of a pickle and mostly of her own making. Anyway, here are some thoughts I might share if we had a cup of tea together.

Let's start with slogans. Crafting a soundbite is not the same as leadership. Wanting a headline grabbing strapline to repeat endlessly, is fabulously easy compared to the grind and graft of implementing your ideas. Your predecessor was also mightily tedious in this regard, but leadership is about doing not spinning. Without achievement, it is not only the slogans that look hollow. Leadership therefore is to selflessly lay foundations on which others may build. If you want to be a columnist or a commentator, feel free to create straplines and slogans to your heart's content; but if you want to lead, you have to build.

Humility is not weakness. If you were elected in part because of your attack lines on your former colleagues, it should not be a surprise to you if they are indifferent or hostile when things are not going well for you. If you have created the atmosphere where people are less likely to help you at the time of your greatest need, then you are the one who needs to change. We might all reflect on how we alienate people with words and deeds (or no words and no deeds). If you lead, you must gather people around, don't push them away or leave them wondering if you care.

Not all experts are right, and even good advisors will sometimes get things wrong, but if you have not listened to experts who have experience and insight you make yourself look isolated and foolish when things turn against you. It is always better to have experts around you who might sometimes get things wrong, than to have experts against you because you rubbished their ideas, especially when they will have the blessing of hindsight when they choose the most uncomfortable time to share their opinions.

Standing by someone, in this case for example your Chancellor, when they have made a monumental mess of their first set piece intervention, is admirable in many ways. Loyalty is important, however set against the peremptory sacking of a key Treasury civil servant and the assertion that broadly not much is wrong, suggests you have not actually understood what is happening or you hope to bluff it out. This is a calamitous plan. "It was the iceberg's fault" is a thin defence when the ship is sinking under your captaincy.

Your big ideas may have merit. You may have waited all your political life to share them. You may be bursting to get on with them, BUT context is everything. A comedian may have the best joke in the world but if they burst into a funeral and regale the mourners with the brilliance of their wit, we might anticipate that the joke will land poorly.

Leadership is trying to do the greatest good for the greatest number. We all matter, not just your most ardent cheerleaders. Your job is to govern the whole country, to reassure us and to leave everyone with a sense of competence so that we can get on with our lives. If you treat the first few weeks of your time in office like trolly dash down the wine aisle with your best mates cheering you on, you risk becoming detached from everyday reality and finding yourself caught up in a world where sycophants, empty drones and vested interests hold too much sway.

We should all focus on what our teams need from us in order for them to succeed. In the UK right now, most people are worried about the cost of living, their energy bills, climate change and the war in Europe. If the things your Ministers want to talk about involve small boats landing on Kent beaches, or whether the BBC is impartial you should not be surprised if voters do not think you are talking to them. And if your ministers say daft things at your annual conference to a small, agitated faction within your tribe, we can of course all hear what they say. Dreaming of sending a few poor souls to Rwanda is perhaps not something to share out loud when the country might prefer you to be more exercised by how many people rely on foodbanks to feed their families.

Ironically most people want you to succeed. It is no fun to be governed by people we don't much like or rate. I suspect most voters just want sensible normal politicians who seem to know what to do. We are broadly not very revolutionary in temperament and would prefer not to be bothered by what you do. Getting on with it would be a start, but if you continue spinning in ever decreasing circles then this is how it will end.

Leadership is hard. We are all poorly equipped when it arrives. In addition, your ideas, your approach, and your strengths, are all largely unknown to us. We need you to reflect, listen and earn our trust. No leader landing suddenly and unexpectedly has an easy time, but they will make it harder for themselves if they choose to plough on without checking if their people are with them.

Finally, it is so easy to criticise and your job is unbelievably hard; so, I do wish you well and I do hope you get better at being our PM. If I may I will finish on a familiar theme for me. Sometimes less is more.

Sometimes small things count more than headlines. You are now in the swirl of a dust storm of your own making. Talk to us and be kind. Right now, I see no kindness in your approach and in those around you. You need no budget for kindness, it does not cost a penny. When money is short, kindness is the first and best resource you can go to. It does not run out; indeed it will only grow with use and it always, always pays back. Be kind, it will help.

Above all, we must do no harm

I had a very vivid and terrible dream last week. It was in fact a truly dystopian nightmare and no fun at all.

I dreamt that I was an enabler for a legal profession that had properly fucked up justice, fucked up any meaningful sense of ethics and fucked up saving the planet. Lawyers had become facsimile lobbyists and plausible apologists for those destroying the planet. We had become a profession that had swapped professional independence for arch indifference and found an ally in sophistry to cloak our eyes from the crimes of our clients.

In my dream I was at a Hollywood-esque awards ceremony and surrounded by brilliant billionaire lawyers. The emerging theme of the evening was that we could make anyone, break anyone, and do anything we liked for whoever we liked. We could do this because we were the special ones, self-anointed in our own infallible judgement and dripping in the obsequiousness of our success.

Acceptance speech after acceptance speech celebrated the breaking down of cultures, traditions and societal norms to release the power of self-interest. There was no irony, no self-awareness and above all no accountability.

Lawyers in this grim universe were not above the law, but outside of it. They were self-appointed puppet masters, one hand guiding the unimaginably rich and the terrifyingly powerful, the other hand holding their noses.

Rules and laws were respected, of course, because that was the game. You had to know the law brilliantly in order to know how it might not apply to anything your clients wanted to do. But then, should a law become just a little bit too inconvenient, the fee for lobbying and promoting a change to the law was even more valuable.

In this nightmare I was sat next to lawyers drunk on arrogance, but their words were also utterly reasonable, measured and knowing. The secret of their success revealed in subtle, but obvious behavioural tics.

These lawyers, of course, would never lie. However, they knew that distraction, diversion and a total command of language was key.

These lawyers, of course, would never cover anything up. However, legal privilege and confidentiality were their legitimate tools often deliberately misunderstood, so that in combination with a limitless client budget, their clients' rights became the expedient lubrication for delay and obfuscation.

These lawyers, of course, would never take any steps against an opponent that they should not take. However, they would casually summon up the grotesque reputations of those they represented, as a service to their opponents who might not otherwise fully comprehend the ferociousness and fear the fight might unleash upon them.

These lawyers, of course, knew that they could not defend the indefensible. However, they would represent anyone over anything, and let the justice system and their clients wealth, test the boundaries of expediency and the limits of their opposers resources.

As communities burned, as institutions failed and as the planet lost its grip on sustainable living, these lawyers celebrated their immunity from scrutiny because they were the keepers of ethicality.

How dare anyone challenge them or their clients' rights to have access to the full power and majesty of the law.

Bloated on their windfall fees, these lawyers did not have to see the consequences of their clients' actions. These lawyers wore this wilful blindfold uncaring that principles that once protected us all, were now only used to cheat humanity and all we had achieved as a society.

My nightmare evening ended with an award for me. For a lifetime of turning the other way. My citation was read to pompous appreciation. The line that jolted me back into consciousness and out of this terrible dream, was this:

"For his unwavering support for our ethical rules that permit us all to sleep well at night. We all know that without our ethical rules, it would be impossible for us achieve anything we have celebrated here this evening."

I sat in my chair as the room then rose in standing acclamation for my contribution to their success. I was unable to move under the burden of knowing that I had resolutely defended ethical rules that had given permission for all these hellish things to unleashed on all of us.

But thank goodness it was just a dream.

It was 3am and I was now wide awake in my hotel room, deeply, deeply disturbed by my dream. Palms sweating and my body shivering with the threat of what my mind had turned over; I did not want to go back to sleep in case I returned to the nightmare. So, I made a cup of tea and I wrote this blog, hugely, hugely relieved that my dream was not real.

I hope to goodness that we will never, ever become so bent out of shape that we see our ethics as a means to exploit situations for our own success. But, perhaps the time has come to add one more line to our guiding rules:

"...and that above all, we must do no harm".

The ODPS System explained

I would like to share something with you that might transform the way you work (aka marketing-speak for something modest that might change things a little bit).

This is a Workflow Management Tool that I have personally developed over decades of real-world, real-time experience. It is not infallible, but anecdotal results suggest that for many people the outcomes vary from "it was fun for a few minutes" to "it saved my career."

I am calling it the OD Paradigm Shift, or the "ODPS System" to make it sound more, you know, pucker. I am now making it freely available for everyone to use.

Typical scenarios when it is helpful to deploy the ODPS System, include:

- When you are presented with a draft contract just before it is due to be signed and asked to "cast an eye."
- When you are asked to approve advertising copy that is about to be published.
- When you receive a meeting request, but with no context, explanation and at short notice, or
- When you take a call from a colleague who says, "I am running this project and someone reckons I need regulatory approval, can you get that for me today or tomorrow ideally?"
- There will be countless other similar situations, but you get the picture.

Now, in the past, when I was in the thick of having a proper job, my reactions to such requests involved plenty of passive aggressive micro-behaviours, a well-developed sense of professional irritation and a slightly depressing acceptance that I would quite quickly say "sure, of course, let me see what I can do."

Three things inevitably follow in these situations. First, our plans for the day are often messed up. Second, we will try to do our best to help. Third, our colleagues learn that we are a soft touch, with time on our hands, and that legal work cannot be that complicated. However, I then learned to deploy the the ODPS System and it was a game-changer for me.

Before describing how to use the ODPS System, it is important to learn how to behave when using it, because the way it is used will undoubtedly enhance the results.

Your body-language must be open, relaxed and super empathetic. You must really listen and convey a sense of profound care for the individual so that whatever they say to you, you will not be irritated. You must then play back to them the key messages shared with you to show you have fully appreciated their problem. In doing so, remember you must show no frustration, but keep smiling and be super friendly.

Then, and this is absolutely critical to the successful deployment of the ODPS System, you must now feign a profound sense of sorrow and disappointment. You might need to practice this to get it right, but it is essential to get this bit right.

It is now that you deploy the ODPS System.

First, you say, "Oh dear" and look sad. Make sure you have eye contact, but say nothing else. Perhaps audibly exhale a little and imperceptibly shake your head, still looking really sad. Your colleague will then sometimes say "Oh dear?" back to you, but with an inflexion as if it has become a question.

Still say nothing. Silence is your friend here. The most likely next comment from your colleague is something like "does that mean you can't help me?"

The Oh Dear Paradigm Shift System is now moving. At this point you say to your colleague, "I am so sorry, but what can you do?".

From here, the conversation may move in all manner of directions, but crucially the "shift" part of the ODPS System has happened. The problem has not been passed painlessly to you, and it remains on your colleague's side of the table, while you have time to think. In my experience (and I accept that this is anecdotal and not empirically tested) 80% of what is presented to you as urgent, suddenly becomes a little less urgent. Indeed around 20% of what is presented to you may disappear altogether. Critically, however, you now have a little more control of things and a little more space to think about what to do for the best.

For more advanced users there are "add-on" features where, for example, you might say to your colleagues, "Let's talk soon about how the way you are working is perhaps unnecessarily increasing your stress levels"

The ODPS System is free to use with my good wishes. Its underlying architecture is robust and relies on three moments of self-awareness:

- You should not allow other people to export their inefficiency.
- You should not allow great service to be conflated with subservience.
- You must recognise that it is partially your fault if other people disrespect your time.
- Your job is to serve the needs of the organisation that employs you, it is not your job to try and meet the day-to-day whims and wants of everyone who drops stuff in your inbox.

Equally however, there is no need to be a grumpy passive-aggressive arse. Some things really are urgent, and some people sometimes don't know what is involved in what they are asking for. The ODPS System is not an excuse for not helping, but it may help you detect those who have not given quite the care to things that would be helpful.

I hope you may use the Oh Dear Paradigm Shift System really well and that it may bring you a little joy and space in your busy lives.

Where are you from?

"You can be anything you want if you work hard enough" is one of the most demoralising, tin-eared and undermining self-help mantras ever contrived.

I assume it is meant as an encouraging remark to inspire our dreams, but to me it says that if you feel left behind, or if your potential has been unrecognised, or if role models are not always visible to you, then perhaps you didn't want it enough or try hard enough.

What no one who is super successful in business ever seems to say is that their journey started with someone recognising that they might have certain gifts and then a small army of people invested in their success by opening up networks and resources to encourage and support their early years.

As small children, if we are told we can walk in space, or win an Olympic medal, or become prime minister, this is wonderful and charming. However, if you are an exhausted adult (perhaps with chain-clanging debt, a hyperactive inner critic and caring responsibilities) and you are told the world is still our oyster if only we seize the moment and work really hard, well that's just unnecessary and unkind. For many people, their ambition is simply to get through the week; and we should see this as a far greater triumph than most of us will ever understand.

Last week the inestimable Richard Moorhead shared a post on his Lawyer Watch blog about class and how it might play out in terms of career opportunities (https://lawyerwatch.wordpress.com/). Like Richard, I was a comp-ed and first-gen university person too. My school was a secondary modern before it became a comprehensive when my year joined. It meant everyone above us thought we were too clever for our own good, and fair game for bullying; while the teachers were just relieved if we turned up and didn't throw chairs at them.

The real battle however was between my low confidence and the school's low expectations. Mum and dad were lovely, but they didn't know I needed help and I didn't know how to ask.

A-levels were a disappointment, and my university offers fell away. I then had an offer to go to Wolverhampton Polytechnic through the clearing system, and I accepted their offer without even visiting the campus. I figured that if this was the only train leaving town, I needed to be on it wherever it was going.

As it turned out I enjoyed my time there very much (I even saw U2 in my first term in the Student Union and have loved the band ever since). I loved learning and loved the diversity of the place. I was beginning to understand myself and I felt I wanted to qualify as a lawyer. Getting into the profession however was then another tough and demoralising experience, because no one saw me, they just saw my grades. No one cared to see if there might be story to be told; all they could tell me (if they even replied) was that I was below average in everything and not for them. That was until a member of the teaching staff took a life changing interest in me and got me an interview with a friend's high street law firm in rural Worcestershire. I was offered a training contract and I was on my way.

The sad thing however is that then and now, and at every point in between, despite General Counsel roles in major companies and representative roles on boards and councils, I have never felt that I truly belonged. I have always felt like I slipped through the barriers when I wasn't supposed to get in. Like sitting in the theatre without the right ticket, it could only be a matter of time before I was asked to leave. Despite so many wonderful friendships and supporters, there have also been a few people who have undermined me and challenged me, and it is their words that sting forever. They sting so much because I never fought back. I passively accepted their unpleasantness because (in my mind) they had stumbled on a truth that I had been trying to hide.

I think this is why the question of where we come from matters so much. It is never, ever just about working hard and wanting something enough.

Well-meaning inclusion and social mobility policies are a beautiful start, but it isn't just about being included, it is also about being helped with one's (often) self-inflicted insecurity. I think this is why I am drawn to mentoring and why I know it is such a privilege to find the stories in other people. The profession is amazing in so many ways, but too often it crushes vulnerability without even realising.

I know this to be true, that we don't all start in the same place; so that even if we seemingly arrive at the same place, how we feel at that moment is informed by our beginning and that will last forever.

"If you want something badly enough and work hard, you can be anything you want" is just bollocks, isn't it?

The older I get, the more I see that everyone has their struggle and that everyone has their amazing story too. All our stories are only partially told and there is always so much more to be explored and treasured.

When I pause with someone to listen to their story, and if I can be a small part of their story to come, what a privilege and a gift that is for me.

And what a blessing it will be if together we all gain from the kindness of listening to each other and from paying attention to all our stories.

November 2022:

It's about being strategic, innit?!

On Friday evening I was driving back from Cambridge after one of our residential alumni events with some of our friends who have completed our leadership programme or who have worked with us as "wise owl" mentors. We had just spent 24 hours together reflecting on what it means to be strategic. With nearly three hours on the motorway to get through and the unrelenting misery of radio news programmes spoiling my mood, I opted for silence and a chance to properly reflect on the things discussed when brilliant people, with big hearts and generous spirits share some time together.

For much of my working life it has been a familiar refrain of lawyers that they would like to be "more strategic." In part this is a plea to do less routine, mundane work, and partly a desire to sit in more important meetings. This ambition, however, is rarely described in terms of the difference this would make.

It may seem a little harsh to say so, but any ambition which is described by what it isn't, is more likely to remain unfulfilled. Saying, "I don't want to do the boring stuff anymore" is not necessarily a compelling reason for your credentials to be able to do anything else.

There are however some uncomfortable dead-ends which some of us, me included, once hoped might be a fast track to becoming more strategic, but which became a slow road to operational mediocrity.

For example, business partnering is not being strategic. It mostly means you are at the beck and call of people who consider you to be "their lawyer." You'll get little credit for making them look great, and your role will become one of willing subservience. Being proactive is not being strategic. It mostly means you will attend more meetings than you need to, that you will feel overwhelmed at how easy it is for other people to give you work, and how little you can complain because it was what you apparently asked for and wanted. Working all hours is not being strategic. It is mostly a product of business partnering and being proactive. It will burn up your well-being and in the end it doesn't make one jot of difference. And, having a reputation for fighting fires, even if you do it brilliantly, is not being strategic. A crisis can be validating, even enjoyable; but it encourages short-term, reactive thinking and gives everyone an excuse not to tackle planning for change that might actually make life easier and better. Even if you achieve executive status it does not mean you are, or will become, strategic because being strategic isn't determined by status or hierarchy or resources.

So, what is it then?

Being strategic is about how you think, how you plan, how you build relationships and how you assess the contribution that you need to make.

Being strategic is having such clarity and simplicity of objective that your team and your business understand it and support it. Being strategic is then having clarity in your planning and having the relationships in place to get the job done.

Being strategic is building those relationships before you need them. You can invest in many things, from tech to process improvement, to operating models, but your relationships are the key to everything positive. No conversation should ever be wasted. Never cancel a one-to-one. Be a great listener, be a generous mentor, and care about your people deeply and genuinely.

Being strategic is also ensuring you have a compelling narrative for your objective; so that simplicity, clarity and integrity should flow through every single word.

Then you must plan together with your team, being open to all ideas and perspectives. Delegate as much as you can to release your team's energy, passions, care and creativity. Test their ideas, and then bring everyone towards the settled course of action, before it is then implemented with kindness, open-mindedness and determination.

In doing so, you must also free yourself (and others) of those things that undermine your objective; give yourself time to encourage your colleagues and be open to how you can flex your plan to keep the objective in your sights and on track.

Being strategic is the power of influence aligned to the talent of your team and the needs of the moment. It is leadership stripped of status distractions and steeped in kindness, openness, vulnerability and determination to do what is right, right now.

You can be strategic too. We don't have to wait for strategic status to be bestowed upon us; it isn't exclusive to those of higher rank, and it is never just about being in "big" meetings. We can all be strategic and we all need to be.

Seeing the good for the trees

I was sat in the back of a large and comfortable car, picked up from the airport and now heading to an important meeting on a remote private estate. Once we were clear of the airport's concrete profile we were quickly into forest with glimpses of lakes between the trees. As we headed deeper and deeper into November's wet gloom, I noticed the driver's grip on the steering wheel tighten a little as wind-slapped rain slowed and buffeted our way. I also noticed how the windscreen-wipers made that comforting metronomic sound as if the car had a heartbeat.

These moments are made for noticing and reflection. I wondered how a little boy from a small town in Wiltshire found himself being chauffeured through a Swedish forest to a secretive location? A boy once frightened of his own shadow, and who's dreams were once compressed by a careers talk at school where a whole school year was told that girls could be hairdressers and boys could join the army. I had flown into Gothenburg already feeling very reflective. The day before I had been with a wonderful client who was trying to come to terms with some life-changing family news. It would be fair to say I was thinking much more about her and her family than the meeting ahead of me.

The trees of the forest were taller now and more densely packed. I had little clue where I was heading and I was becoming a little anxious about how I would appear to my new clients. I wasn't sure if I had the energy to make a difference to their corporate needs. These people were the global leadership team of senior lawyers and compliance professionals for a world-renowned brand. I was tired, distracted and slightly careworn, and I might not be half as good as this new client was expecting.

My car swept up a long drive where the gravel was cinematically deep, making that satisfying sound of tyres crunching stones that you just know would be emphasised by any director if this was a film. The main building of this small estate was a beautifully elegant lakeside manor house – a little tired, but gracefully so. In France it would be a modest but classy chateau. In England it would be the home to an ancestral family with baggy jumpers and more dogs than children, but not of Dukes or endowed to the National Trust.

The space for our meeting was a converted outbuilding. Here there were the familiar clues of a strategic corporate mindset. There was a large horseshoe shaped board table facing two imposing wall-mounted LED screens and generally a sense of big business with its tie off, but its jacket still on. It was quietly understated, but solidly confident in status and permanency. Such rooms, with the slight whiff of leviathan, can still fold my confidence into a pocket square.

As the time came for me to speak, expectant faces looked upon me, and my mouth obviously dried at the very moment when I knew I must say something. I let their silence roll towards me, until it lapped around my thoughts. This silence is a place I know well. It allows me to start gently, no need for faux theatrics; and so it began, a chance for me to explore the needs of the people in this room.

Corporate tones are often our armour. They offer identity, a shared history, a binding vocabulary and values we (hopefully) believe to be well meant and real. But in every team there will be thoughts that sit just below these surface tones – where people are separated from families (even if only temporarily), worried for loved ones, anxious for colleagues and sometimes for themselves. There will be hidden stories, uncertainties, pressures from change, pressure from low confidence, and the pressure of fitting in when other aspects of life are bent out of shape. No team of individual people is ever exclusively an avatar of their brand, however intimidating the table they sit behind.

Our time together passed quickly and I see things differently now. I know I have found a tribe of inspiring individuals. People who care enough about each other to have written a song for a retired colleague, a team who hug and care about what they must do, but above all they care about how they must be. I found a group who listen and challenge, and who liked the space we created together for conversation and reflection; people who have an understated eloquence about their value and their humanity.

I think there is a universal truth in such moments as these. When we give our time to people, we must give them all of the time that we have offered. This is to focus on them, to listen to them, to build with them and to create a memory with them. This is the greatest gift that time can bestow. It might only be for a few minutes, but if we can give our time unconditionally and exclusively, it respects everyone and offers the chance for everyone to be heard. This team gave me the gift of their time and I felt privileged to be part of a small memory that we created together for all of us.

The next day I was driven back to the airport, the rain still falling. This time I shared the car with one of the lawyers who was also catching her flight home. We chatted about travel and meetings but also about her children and how she couldn't wait for her youngest to run into her arms later that day. How lucky am I to have that moment when I was confirmed in the certainty that the very best teams are not just intellects in large leather chairs; because teams only become great when they become aware of the depth, richness and soulfulness of their individual humanity.

You are the architect of your future, not the tenant of your past

Someone asked me last week "how do I fulfil my potential?"

My answer may have lacked a little in hard-nosed strategy, and perhaps suggested that I had seen far too many "inspirational" posters with sunrises or eagles soaring over mountains. However, I could not bring myself to talk of finding a high-performance culture, or of stretch targets, or profile-raising networking, or of writing a more compelling Linked-in profile; instead, I said, "You will fulfil your potential when you find the joy in your work."

I do not believe we are fulfilled (for long) by status or role titles, or by the brands that employ us temporarily for now, or in what we are paid. These things appeal to our inner trinket hoarding magpie, but not to what makes us feel truly fulfilled. I believe we are fulfilled when we make our difference, when we feel heard and when we believe that making our difference has an essential connection with our character and values, and is not just a casual correlation with our to-do list. I believe it is about finding joy in the gifts that are uniquely ours, and then using those gifts to make our mark on the world.

Let me share with you the conundrum of the so called "career path." There isn't ever a path that is visibly unfurled in front of us. The only path that is visible is the one behind us. From where we stand, looking back we can see our hopes and dreams, some achieved, some cast aside; but when we look forward our next step is neither certain nor real until it is made. It is as if we are perpetually on the edge of darkness. We know that it might be wonderful, or challenging, or even a wrong turn, but life's unpredictability and our unique mix of hope, ambition and fickle confidence, will cloak our view. We stand at the entrance to a cathedral of possibility, but we are in the dark.

There is a reason for the darkness; it is to discourage us from staring in vain at uncertainty. When we illuminate our present, we see more of our potential than we ever will by spending time peering into a shrouded future of what-ifs and maybes. Our potential is not something we can order to be delivered on a future date, like a parcel of fulfilment waiting in a depot for a van and a bar code to be scanned. Potential is what we find when we decide to occupy the here and now.

One of the lines I often use in my work is that we should be "the architects of our future and not the tenants of our past." I say it so predictably that in some of my presentations I am sure a few people now finish the sentence for me. However, it isn't just a nice line to pop into a talk, for me it goes to the heart of my work.

We are not trapped by our past, because now does not have a past. Neither can we be certain of a glorious future, because now is all that we have for sure. However, because we have now, with its foundations of experience and expertise, and because we have the tools of kindness, hope, generosity and care, we can make now better. To make something better is joyful and to use our gifts well is to fulfil our potential.

The way forward will never be clear, but our past does not constrain us if we decide to use our gifts to shine our light in the present. When we let go of what the future might be, we can focus on making now kinder, more thoughtful, more hopeful, more loving and more secure. When we look to meet the needs of others, and ask others to help us meet our needs, then fulfilment is possible in the joy of knowing we did what the moment needed us to do and what the moment needed us to be.

We can all take a wrong turn in a career; we can all find ourselves in places that do not value us as we would hope. In a career of thirty or forty years, it will be impossible not to have moments of great stress and regret. However, we always have now to make a difference. Our potential is not in a job, or a brand, a grade or a reporting line; our potential is in the joy we find in today.

If this sounds all too wishy-washy and jars with your reality, and I get that it might, please just ask yourself what harm will ever come from being kinder, listening better, supporting more and also asking for help when we need it? I understand that you may have been through a horrible period and your confidence is low, but the way back to finding the best of you is to stay close to the moment and to make the difference you can. Alternatively you may be on a leadership fast-track superstar grid; but if you are a knob, you will never know the full extent of the difference you could make.

I hope your career path is decorated with care and pride in all that you achieve. I hope your potential is always fulfilled by finding some joy in each and every day. The future will be what it will be, but whoever we are, wherever we are and whatever we are – none of us are the tenants of our past, and all of us can be architects of our future when we decide to light up the moment and shine.

On our watch, our scandal

I try not to give advice, I try mostly to help people find their own way, rather than to follow mine. However, if there was one universal note I would give to any lawyer, anywhere in the world, it would be this:

"Never leave a meeting regretting what you did not say. Always leave a meeting wondering if what you did say could have been said better."

This is not a superficial nod in the direction of better comms; for me this goes to the very heart of our role. It is the existential essence of us.

To speak up when it is expedient to stay silent is neither easy nor always safe. To risk revealing our lack of understanding is courageous when negative judgements about us will be made in an instant. To stand aside from the cheer-leading momentum in the room and to ask "Are we sure? or "Yes, but" is hard. In doing so, we know we will look less than the team player or business partner that the easy clichés encourage us to be.

We all know our duty, but some people I meet lack a curiosity about their roles. They are breathtakingly clever for sure, and undeniably able and successful, but they are also strangely inert and un-noticing about how to make their difference more effectively. They seem to lean on their talent and rest. Other people I meet, clearly care deeply about their contribution, but feel overwhelmed by all that they are asked to do; and in so doing they lose sight of what it is that they must do. It is as if they are always swimming against the tide, with undercurrents of demand that may pull them under at any time.

We all know our duty, but for very different reasons, these lawyers may find that hindsight is a rather judgemental critic. I don't want this to sound harsh or judgemental myself, but this is simply not good enough. Every lawyer knows what they must do in order to fulfil their duty.

Two weeks ago, I stood in an upstairs room of the Frontline Club in Paddington, London surrounded by super-heroes. Men and women, the victims of the Post Office Scandal, hugging each other, checking up on each other, listening to each other. Also in the room were many of the extraordinary legal team that so diligently and courageously fought for their stories to be heard. The gathering was for the paperback launch of the updated "The Great Post Office Scandal" written by Nick Wallis.

One of the sub-postmasters, Vipin Patel, shared a little of his story. He told us of the awful and all too familiar accusations, and of his prosecution. He told us of the money he was accused of taking and of a life broken by the injustice. While we must never get used to hearing these stories, what has stayed with me was not the detail of the case against him, but how Vipin was so gentle, vulnerable and ordinary. Here was a man of soft tones, hesitant in the limelight, but full of dignity and sorrow. Here was a man who wasn't sure what on Earth had happened to him; and someone who felt shame and anguish in a bewildered, helpless kind of way. He could have been my dad. He could have been your dad.

This is what is so unfathomable for me. I do not believe that any lawyer in the world who had met Vipin, who had heard him speak and saw his broken heart, could not have a question about his capacity to be dishonest or his capability to steal. Did no-one meet him, talk with him, hear him? Read about him? Wonder about him? Did the lawyers involved never ask the questions "Are we sure?" or "Yes, but?"

Did it never cross their minds in all the meetings that must have happened about his case that something might not be right?

"Never leave a meeting regretting what you did not say. Always leave a meeting wondering if what you did say could have been said better."

The tragedy of the Post Office Scandal is etched in the faces of the sub-postmasters and their families. It is an historic failure of our justice system, an historic failure of corporate governance and an historic failure of lawyers resting on their talent or perhaps just too busy to see.

The scandal is also mine and yours for every time we did not speak up or did not speak up well enough.

We must all own this if we are to live up to our duty, and not just live up to our privilege. We must all own this if it is not to be an abstract bad thing that happened to other people far, far away from our reality. We must all own this if people like Vipin are not to be persecuted by clever lawyers whose duty to their careers has become greater than their duty to justice.

It happened on our watch; this is our scandal.

The book "The Great Post Office Scandal" by Nick Wallis is now available in paperback from Bath Publishing. Please read it. Please pass it on. Please always speak up and speak well.

If sadness casts a shadow in the sun's low light

Last week I spent four days in North Cornwall. A place blessed in beauty all year round, but which in late November has a stripped back, brooding quality revealed in monumental shadows as sea breezes move the sun's low light across glorious views, but without carrying any of its warmth.

I have needed a break from work for a little while. Tiredness has accumulated in the nooks and crannies of my mind and body, and it has felt harder to be at peace with all my spinning thoughts that never seem to find their place to rest for long.

Cornwall is one of the places I feel I can lie low beneath the persistent hum of task-lists and agendas. It is a place where I only need to focus on how many layers of clothing to wear and to make sure that I lift my head to see and feel those stunning views.

As life slowed down and work drifted to a less pressing priority, I was relieved to find that there was still so much joy in the canvass-ready seascapes and in the sound of waves rhythmically moving their haul of sand and pebbles up and down the beach with each crashing fall; but I also noticed that despite the season-changing soulfulness of this place, I continued to carry the weight of underlying sadness that I could not quite put down.

Perhaps, I quietly counselled myself, I must acknowledge that for now at least there is more for me to accept about how I am feeling than just some accumulated work fatigue.

I do not say this lightly, and I do not say it to suggest that we are all the same, but I know that sometimes I hope to fix what makes me sad with a treat, or a drink with a friend, or a little break from all that is normal. Sometimes however I know that this is only a distraction and, back in my real world, it fixes nothing.

I am too old and too gnarly and too set in my ways to try new things, but one thing I have always tried to do is to accept that whatever beckons a low mood to stand at my side and to pull at my sleeve, it is just as much a part of me as the things that make me laugh, or feel love or which allows for tears of joy.

I didn't need my break in Cornwall to fix my sadness, but I did need it to remind me that my sadness is part of me and should always be allowed to stand beside me. It will not always pull at my sleeve, but when it does there is still joy and beauty in this world to seek out and love.

My sadness therefore is not a darkness that drapes over joy; my sadness is the shading that lets the joy have more definition within my familiar routines. I am grateful for it, as I am grateful for my time in Cornwall and the reminder it gave me that my sadness is not to be fixed like some work-based project. My sadness is just the shadow that let's me know the sun is still shining.

Acceptance

This is a time of year that arrives with mixed blessings for so many. A time when feelings about what has been lost push their way to the surface again; and a time when the weight of expectation rather rudely leans on our efforts and stares, arms folded, at our less than perfect realities. A time when we all try to navigate each day neither wanting to dampen the mood for anyone else, nor reveal our own doubts about how we are coping. It is a time when, in the same moment, we can feel the warmth of togetherness and still note the chill left by someone who is no longer there to hug and hold.

I arrive at the year end with a bag full of thoughts that I have collected along the way. One of which is that the older I get the more aware I am of my shortcomings, but also the more grateful I am for every moment when I am accepted for having them. This isn't something I take lightly or assume is deserved, but it is very special. I also note, for example, that for most of my adult life, and I suspect yours, one of the obligations placed on us has been to develop and to seek continuous improvement. We talk a lot of personal development and professional development. I wonder however if there is an equally valid and important idea that we have under-valued more than we should. Could there be something for us that is vital in a feeling of personal acceptance and professional acceptance?

I do not mean that we should be happy with incompetence or celebrate inertia, but to constantly strive is exhausting and reducing. Perhaps knowing when to let go of developing and to just be ourselves is the best way we can replenish the energy we need in order to move forward again. In the same way, perhaps knowing when to say to our teams "You've done great, let's enjoy this period when we don't have to fight for everything" might be a gift of unexplored riches.

Even more importantly, I wonder if acceptance is the first step in being truly inclusive. If all our vocabulary at work is about change, transformation, improvement and progression, what message is heard by those who feel outside, or left behind, or who wonder if they will ever be good enough, or who feel that their vulnerability has to be protected not exposed?

Acceptance can be our gift to others so that they may feel we truly love who they are and what they bring; it should also be a gift to ourselves because, despite how we sometimes see our place in the world, we are just right, just as we are.

Especially at this time of year, and even more so when we are encouraged to bang down the door of a New Year with empty resolutions, I hope we can pause and reflect on our stories and love that we are all here in our perfect imperfection. I hope acceptance may become a feature of how we love what we have already achieved and honour our individual need not always to strive.

I will always have shortcomings, and I will always fall short of what is ideal, but I also hope so much that I will always be accepted.

Thank you for all your encouragement, your kindness and love this year. Every moment when my words have been noticed, it has helped me to accept myself as well. I am so grateful for the time you give me; it is an honour I receive from you that is beyond words.

With my love and my very best wishes, please take care.

Other books by Paul

All these books can be bought from the
LBC Wise Counsel website: **www.lbcwisecounsel.com**